DELIVERY BY DESIGN

Intermunicipal Contracting, Shared Services,
and Canadian Local Government

ZACHARY SPICER

Delivery by Design

Intermunicipal Contracting, Shared Services, and Canadian Local Government

UNIVERSITY OF TORONTO PRESS
Toronto Buffalo London

© University of Toronto Press 2022
Toronto Buffalo London
utorontopress.com

ISBN 978-1-4875-0524-0 (cloth)
ISBN 978-1-4875-3183-6 (EPUB)
ISBN 978-1-4875-3182-9 (PDF)

___

Library and Archives Canada Cataloguing in Publication

Title: Delivery by design : intermunicipal contracting, shared services, and Canadian local government / Zachary Spicer.
Names: Spicer, Zachary, 1983–, author.
Description: Includes bibliographical references and index.
Identifiers: Canadiana (print) 20220211388 | Canadiana (ebook) 20220211515 | ISBN 9781487505240 (cloth) | ISBN 9781487531836 (EPUB) | ISBN 9781487531829 (PDF)
Subjects: LCSH: Local government – Canada – Management. | LCSH: Intergovernmental cooperation – Canada.
Classification: LCC JS1710 .S65 2022 | DDC 320.80971 – dc23

___

We wish to acknowledge the land on which the University of Toronto Press operates. This land is the traditional territory of the Wendat, the Anishnaabeg, the Haudenosaunee, the Métis, and the Mississaugas of the Credit First Nation.

University of Toronto Press acknowledges the financial assistance to its publishing program of the Canada Council for the Arts and the Ontario Arts Council, an agency of the Government of Ontario.

 Canada Council for the Arts Conseil des Arts du Canada

For Sarah

Contents

List of Figures and Tables   ix
Acknowledgments   xi

1 Introduction   3
2 Mapping the Cooperative Landscape   24
3 Explaining Cooperation   48
4 Agreement Failure and Non-cooperation   77
5 The Role of the Provinces   93
6 Conclusion   101

Appendix   113
Notes   115
References   121
Index   143

Figures and Tables

Figures

2.1 Interlocal Agreements by Policy Area 25
2.2 Local Resources Shared 26
2.3 Interlocal Agreements, 1995–2013 31
2.4 Policy Areas of Interlocal Agreements in the Study 32
2.5 Average Agreement Intensity by Census Metropolitan Area 45
3.1 Reasons to Cooperate 55
3.2 Qualities in Partnership 56
3.3 Characteristics Dissuading Cooperation 57
4.1 Reasons for Agreement Failure 83
4.2 Policy Areas Connected to Agreement Failure 89
5.1 Cooperative Policy Areas, Greater Vancouver Regional District 97

Tables

2.1 Census Metropolitan Areas Chosen for the Study 28
2.2 Interlocal Agreements per Census Metropolitan Area 29
2.3 Components of Interlocal Agreements in the Study 37
2.4 Types of Interlocal Agreements, by Census Metropolitan Area 38
3.1 Conditions for Effective Interlocal Cooperation 50
3.2 Motivations and Incentives of Interlocal Cooperation 51
3.3 Municipal Policy Areas, by Strength of Competition 69

Acknowledgments

This book took several years to bring together, but it would not have seen the light of day without several people and organizations. I would like to acknowledge the financial support of the Social Sciences and Humanities Research Council of Canada, which saw early promise in this project and generously provided funding to collect agreements, complete surveys, and hire research assistants. I would also like to thank the Faculty of Liberal Arts and Professional Studies for further financial support to complete the book when I arrived at York University in July 2021.

An early component of this project involved a full-day workshop at the University of Toronto, hosted by the Institute on Municipal Finance and Governance. Many thanks to Enid Slack and the Institute for their ongoing support. Thank you as well to those who attended and presented at the workshop. Many of the agreements collected for this book were painstakingly obtained by Kate Daley, who provided invaluable research assistance throughout the project. Many thanks for Kate for her amazing work! The Laurier Institute for the Study of Public Opinion and Policy (LISPOP) supported the early design of the survey and assisted me in deploying the survey to municipal administrators across Ontario. Many thanks to LISPOP and, particularly, Andre Perrella for the support!

I would like to thank the Province of Ontario for providing me with data from past surveys, reports, and archival material. Additional thanks to the countless municipalities that provided documentation and the staff who helped along the way. Interview material was critical to bringing this study to publication. Many local administrators generously agreed to speak with me and share information that was accessible in no other way. Because of the research ethics protocols for this project, I cannot thank them by name, but I hope they know how much I appreciate their time and insights.

Finally, Daniel Quinlan at the University of Toronto Press was instrumental in bringing the book together. After pitching him on the idea several years ago, he demonstrated remarkable patience as I worked through several drafts and (slowly) completed revisions. Thank you, Daniel! I would also like to thank freelancer Barry Norris for copyediting the book and JoAnne Burek for preparing the index. A final thank you to everyone at the University of Toronto Press for moving the manuscript quickly through the final editing and production process.

Ultimately, this book, like all my writing, would not be possible without the love and support of my family: Sarah, Jacob, and Kennedy. Thank you for everything!

DELIVERY BY DESIGN

Intermunicipal Contracting, Shared Services,
and Canadian Local Government

1 Introduction

On the outskirts of Sudbury, Ontario, rest four small municipalities: Markstay-Warren, St.-Charles, French River, and Killarney. In total, the four municipalities have approximately 6,600 residents scattered over 3,200 square kilometres. Like most northern and remote communities, a sparse population spread over an immense geography presents a unique set of policy and service delivery challenges. The cost of providing basic municipal services to these populations is massive. Politicians and administrators in the four communities understand these challenges well. Population increases have not occurred regularly and, as provincial grants for servicing support began to dwindle, each municipal government was forced to take a hard look at what it could offer its residents (Kerr 2018).

Municipalities in such a predicament have a number of options at their disposal. One is to limit or restrict servicing options. Certain services are mandated under provincial legislation, but municipalities can adjust service levels to fit their budget. Another option is to use private contracting to deliver services in the hope that this might reduce service expenditures. The municipalities of Markstay-Warren, St.-Charles, French River, and Killarney, however, chose a third option: service sharing, whereby they opted to pool resources and deliver certain services collectively as a way not only to reduce expenditures but also to improve the quality of the services they were offering (Kerr 2018). As a result, residents in these municipalities were able to enjoy relatively stable service levels, as they had in the past, while their governments avoided contracting with private sector entities. In this sense, service sharing represented a collective solution to common public policy challenges.

Although the four Northern Ontario municipalities began with a plan in mind, politicians and administrators from each still did not know exactly how to start the service- sharing process. The four municipalities approached accounting firm KPMG to conduct a study on the possibility of service sharing and contracting. After examining the operations of each municipality, KPMG identified seven potential service areas that could be shared: group purchasing, shared by-law enforcement, regional training, a regional approach for the addition of municipal drainage personnel, creation of engineering/asset management capacity, and a collective equipment maintenance policy (Kerr 2018). KPMG also identified three areas that did not lend themselves well to service sharing given the geography and finances of the region – namely, fire services, senior administration, and economic development (Kerr 2018). With a plan in place from KPMG, the four municipalities moved forward to share the recommended services. They also explored the use of shared fire training and inspection, despite KPMG's objections to service sharing in this area (Kerr 2018).

There were, of course, hurdles to overcome throughout the exploration and implementation process. For instance, Killarney is more than an hour's drive from the other three municipalities, meaning that geographic distance prevented the community from realizing service-sharing benefits in all areas. In fact, during in-depth analysis of service-sharing possibilities it was shown that Killarney's participation, in fact, might have increased the costs of servicing for all four municipalities. As a result, Killarney was allowed to opt out of certain services, while sub-agreements were formed in each service area to create flexibility for each municipality (Kerr 2018).

For Markstay-Warren, St.-Charles, French River, and Killarney, service sharing held a lot of potential for delivering better quality services potentially at a lower price, but there was also a desire to maintain autonomy. "We're distinct municipalities," said Denis Turcot, the Chief Administrative Officer for Markstay-Warren, arguing that there was a strong desire to maintain that distinctiveness and autonomy (Kerr 2018). In the 1990s, municipal amalgamation was forced on the area, and there was little desire to return to such discussions despite the challenges each municipality was experiencing with fiscal health and servicing allowances (Kerr 2018). As such, service sharing offered the possibility of preserving municipal autonomy while exercising service efficiency.

Markstay-Warren, St.-Charles, French River, and Killarney are certainly not alone in exploring the potential benefits of interlocal cooperation and service sharing. In fact, a number of municipalities across Canada have engaged in the same exploratory work. Elsewhere in Ontario, the municipalities of Newmarket, Richmond Hill, Aurora, Markham, Vaughan, and Pickering entered into an agreement to construct and share five water-pumping stations. In Alberta, the City of

Wetaskiwin, the County of Wetaskiwin, and the Town of Millet collaborated on a regional industrial growth plan to address economic development. In Yukon Territory, the Village of Teslin has entered into a series of service-sharing relationships with the Teslin Tlingit Council, an Indigenous band government, in a range of service and policy areas, such as sewer services, a skateboard park, sustainability planning, and recreation. In fact, even Canada's largest city, Toronto, has a multi-million-dollar water-contracting relationship with its northern municipal neighbour, York Region.

Although the enthusiasm for interlocal cooperation is understandable given some of the perceived benefits, there are, of course, a host of reasons municipal decision makers might be wary or hesitant to cooperate. The most obvious is that the other party – or parties, in the case of multilateral agreements – might not honour their end of the arrangement (Matkin and Frederickson 2009). While two municipalities might enter into an agreement in good faith, one municipality could simply refuse to abide by the arrangement over time, leaving the other with immense costs or operational load. Municipalities are, after all, subject to some politically volatility. If an election were to bring in a new council with a new attitude on interlocal arrangements, existing agreements might be terminated, leaving the other parties on the hook. Even if one partner does not terminate the agreement, the cost of monitoring the arrangement or constantly adjusting it to suit a disgruntled partner might erase any savings experienced by first entering into the agreement (Post 2004).

The costs of interlocal agreements also might change over time, as those of materials or labour fluctuate (Kanareck and Baldassare 1996; Williams 1967). These variations could cause a strain on municipal budgets and make long-term budgeting challenging, if not impossible. The quality of the service also might decline over time, leading to arrays of complaints from the general public and the application of political pressure on decision makers to improve or abandon the service (Post 2004). Generally speaking, then, for interlocal cooperation to work, the potential benefits must be high and the transaction costs of coordinating, negotiating, monitoring, and enforcing the arrangement must be low (Lubell et al. 2002). If local decision makers cannot ensure that the costs and risks of partnership will remain low and the conditions for cooperation politically favourable, interlocal cooperation becomes a much less attractive proposition.

The research conducted for this book identified hundreds of municipalities that have some type of municipal service sharing or contracting relationship. These governments have found at least some benefits to cooperation. In Canada, the research also finds, such relationships are not as numerous as in Europe, Asia, or the United States, but they do represent an intriguing departure from traditional models of service delivery and, as such, are worth the attention of those interested in municipal governance, service delivery in local governments, and public policy.

The Calculus of Cooperation in Canada

Municipalities have options when deciding how best to deliver many of their services. One way is to produce and deliver the service independently – an option many municipalities have chosen. For instance, to satisfy residents' demand for curbside trash collection, the local municipal government could purchase garbage trucks and build processing facilities to deliver the service; if public transit is demanded, it could purchase buses, design the network and schedule, and operate the system.

Another option involves other actors, either private firms or other governments, and moves beyond the independent delivery of services. To return to the examples above, if residents demanded curbside waste collection or a transit network, the municipality could contract with a private firm, as some municipalities in North America are doing with ride-hailing services such as Uber (see Siekierska 2018). Under these arrangements, the municipal government is responsible for paying the private firm to produce or deliver (or both) the service in question, thereby eliminating some of the capital or operating costs involved in local service delivery.

I provide more information on the use of private actors in service delivery in subsequent chapters, but the main focus of the book is on interlocal cooperation – that is, cooperation with other governments. Intermunicipal collaboration or contracting occurs where one local government contracts or collaborates with another local government either to produce and deliver a service through a contract or to produce and deliver the service jointly to their residents. Simply put, one municipal government could produce a service jointly with another or contract the other to provide the service on its behalf.

Intermunicipal cooperation is a particularly interesting subject in the areas of public administration and political science in that it takes a number of forms, ranging from simple mutual aid agreements to formalized multi-million-dollar delivery contracts. Although service delivery is generally the focus of local intergovernmental efforts, interlocal cooperation goes beyond servicing. Municipalities can be creative and partner on a range of initiatives from economic development to sharing staff to working together on grant applications to throwing joint community celebrations and festivals. This cooperation can be voluntary or compulsory, formal or informal, and, ultimately, successful or unsuccessful. Examining when, how, and under what conditions municipalities cooperate is an evolving research area, but one that is vitally important to our understanding of the policy and administrative processes of Canadian local government.

Although interlocal contracting and service sharing is an intriguing method for local service delivery, we know comparatively less about the practice in Canada than in other countries. This is not to say that Canadian research on the subject has been sloppy or haphazard, merely that the dearth of research is likely the result of scale. In Europe, Asia, and the United States, groups of researchers have been working for years to better understand the conditions in which cooperative relationships emerge among municipalities. We have not had that luxury in Canada. What can be said, however, is that the research we have in Canada and elsewhere in the world is of sufficient maturity to offer lessons to students, researchers, and municipal practitioners about the causes and consequences of intermunicipal cooperation and institutional design. As such, this book's first contribution is assembling and synthesizing existing research into a straightforward and clear text.

Another goal of this book is to add to our understanding of interlocal cooperation in Canada by assessing the local cooperative landscape. Who is cooperating? What types of services are being shared? I also detail the cooperative process, examining why municipalities cooperate or why they choose not to. The desire to compete and grow feeds into this process, as does a range of political factors that might come into play.

What the reader will not find in this book, however, is a utopian vision of interlocal cooperation, which is only one of the options for service delivery and local policy development, and certainly not a panacea for cost savings, efficiency generation, or service optimization. Under certain conditions, a host of potential benefits might be realized, but there are a number of very significant challenges associated with interlocal cooperation, which I detail throughout the book. Practitioners and researchers are better served by a comparison of the benefits and detriments of interlocal cooperation, rather than digesting an advocacy manual. Ultimately, the aim of the book is to provide a balanced view of the interlocal contracting and shared-services process.

Governing Municipalities and City-Regions

The study of interlocal cooperation is closely related to institutional design and the organization of municipal government. Within an institutional context, municipalities are one part of a local governance network that includes special-purpose bodies, such as school boards and conservation areas, that sometimes have overlapping jurisdictions. Municipalities are also subject to an array of provincial statutes and reporting mechanisms, which limits their ability to act independently in a range of policy areas.

The British North America Act of 1867 established a distribution of powers between the federal and provincial governments that placed responsibility for municipalities with the provinces. This was reinforced during the patriation of the Constitution in 1982. Provincial governments, therefore, control the functions, finances, and even the very existence of local governments within their jurisdiction (Tindal et al. 2013). Each province has a ministry dedicated to municipal affairs and a minister who is responsible for managing the business of local government,[1] and at least one accompanying general law or statute that establishes basic rules for municipalities (Sancton 2011). Provincial governments control the composition of municipal authority, the shape of local boundaries, the scope of servicing responsibility, and the ability of municipalities to raise and spend funds.

Municipal services are funded through a narrow set of revenue tools. Municipalities generally have three main sources of revenue: user fees (recreation fees, parking charges, and so on), transfers from senior levels of government, and property tax (Sancton 2011).[2] Generally, more than half of municipal revenue comes from the property tax (Kitchen 2002; Mintz and Roberts 2006). Calls for more municipal revenue sources have occurred quite often over the years (see Powell 2016; Vander Ploeg 2002; Xuereb 2014), but those serving in provincial governments have not been keen to respond or to grant new taxing authority to municipalities.

Given the constrained nature of municipal governance, it is understandable that some have looked to institutional solutions: can we change the institutional scope of municipalities to increase performance? what is the best way to govern a municipality or region? The institutional context of municipal government has received a significant amount of academic attention over the years. Much of this has focused on what is described as the "metropolitan problem," where a layering of local governments has led to a "duplication of functions" and, inevitably, "organized chaos" (Aligica and Tarko 2012). Therefore, the prevailing logic in municipal institutional design for decades called for a single government that would cover an entire metropolitan area (Gulick 1962; Jones 1942; Studenski 1930). This can be referred to as "traditional" or "consolidationist" thinking, as those favouring this perspective called for the enlargement of certain governments so that their borders inevitably reached the limits of the metropolitan area.

This perspective is certainly not foreign to Canadians. Alberta's two largest cities – Edmonton and Calgary – have undergone several rounds of annexation, slowly moving outward by absorbing adjacent municipalities (LeSage Jr. 2005; Sancton 2011). Saskatoon and Regina, the two largest cities in Saskatchewan, have done the same (Garcea 2005). In Manitoba, Winnipeg has undergone several rounds of institutional change, being converted into a two-tier regional government and then facing a large-scale amalgamation (Higgins 1986; Kiernan and Walker 1983). Ontario has gone through the same process, with the province's county system and separated cities eventually making way for regional government and then a province-wide push for local consolidation (Frisken 2007; Spicer 2016a). Quebec has also experienced a number of rounds of amalgamation in and around Montreal, Quebec City, Longueuil, Hull, Chicoutimi, Sherbrooke, and Trois-Rivières (Sancton 2011). In Atlantic Canada, several communities have undergone amalgamation, the most notable being Halifax (Vojnovic 1998). Most recently, the New Brunswick government announced a series of municipal amalgamations across the province, mostly in rural areas (Poitras 2021).

By the 1970s, consolidationist theories gave way to a host of public choice thinkers who viewed the fragmentation in metropolitan areas as functional (Bish 1971; Bish and Ostrom 1973; Ostrom, Tiebout, and Warren 1961). This group rejected the notion that institutional consolidation was an answer to metropolitan problems, arguing that smaller local units create a governmental marketplace in which citizen-consumers ultimately benefit (Atkins, Dewitt, and Thangavelu 1999). Public choice theorists saw institutional fragmentation as beneficial for effective and efficient service delivery.

In this view, with metropolitan areas akin to marketplaces, monopolistic providers are considered unwelcome and unhelpful (Bish and Ostrom 1973, 17). Multiple sources and jurisdictions create competition, leaving citizens to act as consumers and to select the tax and services ratio that best suits them (20). As a rational-choice-based theory, public choice assumes that individuals are aware of the choices before them. This choice represents a simple dichotomy of voice versus exit: individuals can choose to vote or simply leave (voting with their feet) to a jurisdiction that better represents their favoured tax/services ratio. Similarly, Tiebout (1956) argued that the "consumer-voter" could select a community to live in that best reflects the individual's desire for the provision of public goods. More governing units inevitably result in more variation in public goods, thereby providing more choice for individuals. Although the proponents of public choice do, overall, emphasize "exit" over "voice" as a strategy for citizen-consumers, smaller governing units have demonstrated some increase in citizen representation and participation. A variety of participatory means, such as public meetings, hearings, elections, and direct contact with officials, makes government more accessible for individuals in smaller institutional settings (Bish 2001).

Within such an environment, polycentric thinking envisions a theory of hidden order, where a diverse range of decision makers operate at different scales within the system. Here, there is a clear distinction between a polycentric and a monocentric system: the monopoly over the legitimate exercise of coercive capabilities (Aligica and Tarko 2012). In the consolidationist perspective, residents see one set of decision makers at a central level within the metropolitan area. In a public choice framework, the opposite is true, as decision makers operate independently throughout the region. A polycentric political system, then, is one where "many officials and decision structures are assigned limited and relatively autonomous prerogatives to determine, enforce and alter legal relationships" (Ostrom 1972, cited in McGinnis 1999). Within such a system, no one actor has pure authority; instead, many actors hold authority, but are bound by a guiding set of legal rules and norms.

From an Ostromian-Bloomington school perspective,[3] several components of a polycentric urban system emerge: the existence of many centres for decision making, the existence of a single system of rules (either institutionally or culturally enforced), and the existence of a spontaneous social order as the outcome of an evolutionary competition between different ideas, methods, and ways of life (Aligica and Tarko 2012; Goertz 2007).

In Canada, we likely would not recognize a truly polycentric region as envisioned by scholars like the Ostroms. Even common-pool resources (a key feature of Elinor Ostrom's scholarship) are generally managed by centrally imposed special-purpose bodies. Needless to say, we do not necessarily have to worry about self-governing networks. Provincial governments have taken the role not only of guiding local development and governance, but also of acting as a lingering presence over the decisions local government are able to make. As such, we cannot say for certain what the impact of a classically theorized polycentric region would be in Canada, but many of the fears of consolidationists – namely, the parochialism, the tension, and the disorganization of a fragmented metro area – are present within all areas of provincial decision making when it comes to Canada's city-regions.

The debate about which perspective is best has carried on for decades. With the benefit of time, we have seen that many of the promises stemming from consolidation approaches have failed to materialize (Miljan and Spicer 2015; Sancton 2000; Slack and Bird 2013). With larger municipalities inevitably comes a host of unintended consequences, such as decreased representation and increased servicing costs (Found 2012). Metropolitan areas without any type of organization, as envisioned by public choice advocates, are challenging to govern and often-persistent servicing dilemmas might go unresolved (Downs 1994; Spicer 2014).

A middle ground in the consolidationist–public choice debate emerged in the 1990s. Called "new regionalism," this perspective argued that coordination could be achieved through increased cooperation between governmental units (see, for example, Salet, Thornley, and Kruekels 2003; Savitch and Vogel 1996; Vogel and Harrington 2003). Effective metropolitan governance, new regionalists argued, did not necessarily require consolidation. Nor would it require a truly polycentric region.

Over the past twenty years, new regionalist authors contend, cities have undergone tremendous changes and experienced patterns of activity that transcend political boundaries. Since population growth has gradually shifted from central cities to their surrounding suburbs, new regionalist authors cite corresponding issues such as urban sprawl, declining cities, growth concerns, and economic competition for the increased need for regional cooperation (Savitch and Vogel 2000). Consequently, an integrated approach is necessary to address regional issues that transcend local boundaries. Moreover, the rise of globalization enhances the need for city-regions to be more cohesive and competitive (Kresl 1992).

New regionalists place more emphasis on governance than on government. For new regionalists, government entails relying on formal institutional structures to address policy problems; in contrast, governance addresses metropolitan issues with a variety of means other than formal metropolitan structures (Phares 2009, xi). Broadly defined, the new regionalists view governance as the inclusion of non-political actors in the policy process, typically through networks as opposed to hierarchies (Norris 2001). Thus, new regionalists believe that a variety of voluntary means, which include both governmental and non-governmental private actors, can coordinate metropolitan areas effectively (Norris, Phares, and Zimmerman 2009, 12). Through collaborative networks, these actors can link a region.

A common strain connecting each of these schools of thought, as well as their implementation in Canada, is the long-standing search for efficiency. What is the most efficient way to organize a municipal government? With the promises about consolidation and public choice options going largely unfulfilled in Canada, it should come as little surprise that new regionalist ideas involving interlocal cooperation and agreements have become a popular option for municipal practitioners. As mentioned above, these agreements can be either formal or informal, and can span a range of servicing options from simple information sharing to more complex joint management agreements between municipalities (Dollery, Grant, and Kortt 2012; Henderson 2015; Spicer 2014). Despite some scepticism about the prospects of new regionalist governance mechanisms succeeding in Canadian cities (Frisken 2001; Sancton 2001), municipalities are still cooperating on a range of servicing issues (LeSage Jr., McMillan, and Hepburn 2008; Sancton, James, and Ramsay 2000; Slack 1997).

Much of this interest stems from specific benefits that accrue to local governments. One benefit is financial: sharing a service or contracting with another municipality to provide a service allows a municipality to avoid delivering that service internally. For the most part, this has been accomplished through realizing significant scale economies in certain service areas, which lowers per capita costs for local authorities (Dollery, Grant, and Kortt 2012). These savings, however, tend to be service-specific (Byrnes and Dollery 2002; Dollery, Grant, and Kortt 2012; Fox and Gurley 2006).

Another benefit of local cooperation agreements is that they can fill gaps in service delivery. Simply put, some municipalities are unable to deliver every service they wish (Spicer 2015b) – a municipality that lacks access to sufficient sources of water for its population might seek out neighbouring municipalities to help extend its water service. If a municipality is unable to provide a service independently, there is a good chance it will pursue a cooperative relationship, mainly to overcome geographic or environmental isolation (Warner 2015).

A third benefit is the possibility of increasing the capacity of local service delivery or improving the quality of local services (Post 2004; Warner 2015). This can be accomplished by tapping into the policy expertise of partners or simply by strengthening capacity and resources. The prospect of delivering higher-quality services more efficiently can incentivize the cooperative process.

A fourth benefit of cooperation is the increased ability to control externalities. Within metropolitan areas, policy spillover can be frequent; cooperation can help municipalities better manage externalities and plan for growth, development, and transportation continuity on a regional scale. Cooperative relationships also allow municipalities to monitor shared resources, such as waterways (Post 2004).

Fifth, there is an emerging incentive to pursue local voluntary cooperation in order to promote regionalism. Interlocal service sharing has demonstrated the ability to link a region and provide for policy and service continuity without the need for institutional consolidation. Interlocal cooperation is the most flexible alternative to formal institutional reform, as it allows local governments to decide which regional issues should be addressed collectively (Nelles 2009, 22). The attractive aspect is the possibility of linking a region without sacrificing capacity or autonomy, which some authors have argued allows the local government to remain intact and avoid being "hollowed out" (Hulst and van Montfort 2008).

Finally, municipalities might pursue interlocal cooperative activity to enhance the profile of their community. This largely feeds into the abiding growth ethic of municipal actors, which sees growth as an end in itself (Leo 2002; Leo and Brown 2000). Such boosterism and competition for investment is a long-documented hallmark of city politics (Artibise 1981; Wade 1959), with cities competing for residential, commercial, and industrial development (Binford 1985; Logan and Molotch 1987; Lucy and Phillips 2000; Markusen 1984). Municipalities that are growing rapidly are deemed successful, and are viewed as more desirable to potential residents and businesses (Leo and Anderson 2006). More services of better quality attract more residents and businesses. Cooperative activity can help achieve this goal, although it might diminish the attractiveness of a particular community by enriching a neighbouring municipality.

I delve deeper into the rationale for cooperation later in the book, but for now it is important to understand that interlocal cooperation is a key part of the discussion about efficiency and service production in local government. As Teles (2016, 34) argues, intermunicipal cooperative arrangements are a way of addressing the challenges of suboptimal municipal size and can serve as a functional substitute for territorial consolidation. Many communities might resist consolidation in the hope of preserving their identity (or for a variety of other very justified reasons), but could still encounter challenges regarding scale and efficiency. Interlocal cooperation and contracting could help to meet some of these challenges by maximizing efficiency in service production, while maintaining the institutional composition of the community.

Transaction Costs, Risk, and the Calculation of Reward

While municipalities have a host of reasons available to cooperate with other municipalities on servicing arrangements, cooperation is neither a natural phenomenon nor one without risk. In fact, many municipalities opt to deliver services in-house rather than enter into contractual agreements with other governments that might bind them for significant periods of time or tie them legally to another entity that ultimately might not comply with the arrangement (Feiock 2013). Throughout the process, a municipality gives up some autonomy over a shared or contracted policy area, allowing the other government partner or partners to have some decision-making authority over the level or quality of service delivered (Parks and Oakerson 1989). There is, then, a trade-off between risk and reward.

Generally, cooperation between local governments increases when the potential benefits are high and the costs of coordinating, negotiating, monitoring, and enforcing an arrangement are low (Lubell et al. 2002). Additionally, five groups of core variables influence cooperation between local jurisdictions: social capital, group composition, geographic density, power asymmetry, and political leadership. Although some studies have tested other variables, such as policy control and resource scarcity (Kanareck and Baldassare 1996; Williams 1967), careerism (Matkin and Frederickson 2009; LeRoux and Pandey 2011), and business activity (Johnson and Neiman 2004), the five variables listed above represent the core factors regularly represented in research about interlocal cooperation.

Social capital is a factor that positively affects cooperation (Gulati and Singh 1998; Ostrom 1998). Often, this is derived from social networks or patterns of interaction with others from neighbouring governments (Cook, Hardin, and Levi 2005). Thus, consistent interaction between localities is more likely to result in a positive relationship between both political actors and city staff (Matkin and Frederickson 2009). Their increased interaction familiarizes these actors with one another, eventually leading to the reciprocation of trust, making the emergence of cooperative arrangements more likely.

The composition of any group is another important factor in reaching local agreement. Two areas of group composition, in particular, exert particular influence over cooperation: group size and group homogeneity or heterogeneity. The size of the group determines how benefits can be distributed to members and the transaction costs associated with negotiating and monitoring an agreement. Researchers have found that smaller groups are easier to form and have fewer problems associated with determining the allotment of benefits and monitoring agreements (Post 2004, 74). Larger groups, on the other hand, are harder to organize, produce smaller benefits for members, and create opportunities for some jurisdictions to free ride, which is why research demonstrates that increasing the number of actors in any particular region will limit cooperation (Visser 2004). Additionally, the homogeneity of the actors is important in reaching a cooperative agreement. Post (2004, 84) argues that a decrease in the heterogeneity of the populations served by local governments that enter new agreements is positively related to collective action. As such, a smaller group with a homogenous population will achieve cooperation more easily than a larger group with a more heterogeneous population.

Closely associated with group size is geographic density. For several reasons, geographic density increases the likelihood of cooperation between local governments (Bickers and Stein 2004; Post 2002). For one, the relative closeness of local governments within an area increases the likelihood that residents of one jurisdiction will work in the other and vice versa. Individuals see themselves more as regional citizens and less isolated in one jurisdiction, increasing the pressure on politicians to cooperate with other areas (Post 2004, 73). As well, a higher density of local governments implies greater spillover effects between jurisdictions. Consequently, externalities and economies of scale gradually motivate governing units to cooperate (Shretha and Feiock 2007).

Differences in power are another important variable in determining whether governing units can reach cooperative arrangements. The degree by which prospective partners vary in their power affects the motivation of actors and ultimately determines whether or not the relationship is coercive (Steinacker 2004). In any situation where power asymmetry is great, the stronger actor might exploit the weaker and coerce them into participating in an agreement. Additionally, the relative position of weaker actors might make cooperation a virtual necessity if the stronger actor holds more resources, especially those that are relatively unattainable for the weaker actors without cooperation.

Political leaders also have a large role in initiating and formalizing agreements. Where political leaders have more autonomy to make decisions – and, consequently, are stronger – cooperation is much easier to achieve; however, if a municipal government has very few autonomous areas of jurisdiction, its political leadership might be wary of ceding authority through cooperative arrangements (Alcantara and Nelles 2009). Nevertheless, research demonstrates that strong political leaders can overcome resistance to cooperation from council and various stakeholders (Post 2004) – in general, the presence of strong political leadership in a municipality increases the chances for cooperation.

Transaction costs also affect the formation and outcome of cooperative agreements. Ugboro, Obeng, and Talley (2001, 83) define the transaction costs involved with interlocal cooperation as "the costs of extensive decision making for negotiating, operating and enforcing the provisions of the system." As Feiock (2007) reminds us, such costs must generally be low for any government to explore the possibility of entering into a cooperative or contracting relationship with another government.

Existing research demonstrates four different and identifiable types of transaction costs: information and coordination costs, negotiation and division costs, enforcement and monitoring costs, and agency costs (Feiock 2007, 51). *Coordination costs* refer to the process of identifying opportunities for mutual gain and potential policy partners. Once a potential partner establishes a connection, *negotiation and division costs* are incurred in determining formulas or procedures to allocate an agreement's costs or benefits. This can sometimes be a challenging process. As a result, the conditions under which an agreement was first established can change over the agreement's lifespan, affecting each partner's perceived value and possibly increasing the incentive one partner to renege. *Enforcement costs* derive from efforts to maintain and adhere to the original content of the agreement. And, finally, *agency costs* arise when the preferences of public officials negotiating agreements depart from those of the citizens they represent (Feiock 2002). These transaction costs are not mutually exclusive, as a number of different costs can affect a cooperative arrangement.

In order for interlocal agreements to be of value for participating governments, transaction costs must be overcome. Some transaction costs can be fatal, or act as a drag on the entire project, ultimately inflating the cost of partnership and lessening or even removing altogether any particular efficiency gains from the arrangement. Ultimately, if participating governments cannot recognize a benefit to entering an agreement, they will not cooperate.

Options for Cooperation

Municipalities hoping to pursue local cooperation have a variety of vehicles at their disposal, ranging from informal information sharing to very complex and formalized joint ventures (Feiock 2013). There are, in fact, more than two dozen alternatives to traditional service delivery (Osborne 2000; Parsons 1995). These can be broadly grouped into three categories: contracts, partnerships, or networks (Sullivan and Skelcher 2002; Thompson et al. 1991).

The first, and perhaps simplest, relationship is contractual. Under this type of relationship, a municipality contracts with another to provide a service in its jurisdiction. This is similar to private contracting (see Bel and Costas 2006; Dachis 2010; McDavid 2000), where a private firm either produces or delivers a particular service for a local government in exchange for a set fee. The logic of intermunicipal contracting is very similar: a municipality contracts with another to provide a service, generally for a set fee. More often than not, this involves an exchange of money – an annual or per unit fee (Spicer 2014) – but occasionally it is a service swap of some kind.

Municipalities have a great deal of incentive to contract with municipal governments. They might be experiencing poor fiscal health and cannot afford the capital or operating costs for a particular service, perhaps they lack specialized equipment, such as road works equipment or information and technology infrastructure, or perhaps another municipality has a great deal of policy expertise and experience in a particular area and contracting allows another municipality to tap into it to create better services on an improved policy framework. Generally, if a policy or servicing goal is unreachable alone, cooperation could be a worthwhile endeavour.

Interlocal contracts can be either formal or informal, but formal agreements are by far the norm. Such agreements are legally binding and codified – written contracts that exist on paper and are legally enforceable in courts of law. These are essentially the types of contracts we are most familiar with – the type we might sign when we purchase a home or lease a car. Informal agreements provide an alternative to legally binding contracts (Graddy and Chen 2006). They are unwritten and do not come with the same amount of legal protection and institutional binding, but are open and much more flexible, and are commonly referred to as "handshake agreements" or "oral contracts," in that those making the agreements understand the terms, which are not legally binding.

Little is known about informal contracting at the local level, mainly because information about such agreements is hard to collect. As unwritten arrangements, these contracts cannot be gathered and their components cannot be analysed or systematically compared. In many cases, these informal arrangements exist only in the minds of the individuals who agreed to them, with those from outside the organization having virtually no understanding of the terms or conditions. Needless to say, understanding how informal governance arrangements work in practice poses a number of challenges for researchers; accordingly, I focus instead mainly on formal contracts and agreements.

We do know, however, that the use of informal agreements is sparse (Spicer 2016b). There is some indication that these agreements were used much more frequently in the past, but there has been a trend towards formalization in the past decade, mainly to counter the risks inherent with oral contracts, such as defection, non-payment, and non-compliance (Spicer 2016b). Many of these agreements also might be lost as the staff or politicians who executed them leave the organization and fail to pass along knowledge of the arrangement. There are, however, benefits to using informal service arrangements. They have been shown to lower transaction costs and are relatively flexible, in that municipal actors can exit these arrangements generally without penalty (Spicer 2016b). For some municipalities, short-term servicing relationships with lower dollar values might be preferable, although, as mentioned, these forms of agreements are not widely used.

If the arrangement is formal, the contract lays out the terms of the service, including expectations and a payment schedule. Most contracts differ in size and scope, but they have some commonalities. All contracts will spell out the service in question, and most will have some guidelines for servicing expectations – for example, which service is going to be delivered, who will deliver the service, when the service will be delivered, and to what standard the service will be held. More often than not, a set amount of resources is described, stipulating how much one municipality will pay the other to deliver the agreed-upon service. This is often dictated in terms of a payment schedule – for example, whether the payment is to be made in set periods or when the service is complete or in effect. In general, the contract will set out a term of service, which usually stipulates a set time frame; most extend at least a year, but some can go for more than a decade. There are also often some stipulations for renewal. In some cases, the agreement will be automatically renewed; in others, notification by one or more of the parties must be given to renew the contract.

These formal contracts also often include a termination procedure. If the agreement fails to meet expectations and one party wishes to terminate it, the procedure often includes a set period for notification and occasionally a penalty. In short, these formalized arrangements bind each actor to a certain degree. A formal contract is a legal document and, as such, is enforceable in court. Rarely does a relationship disintegrate to that degree, but formal contracts provide a measure of legal protection for the parties involved.

Why contract with another municipality instead of the private sector? This question is explored in more detail later in the book, but simply put, some municipal actors are unwilling or unable to contract with the private sector. Privatization of nearly every municipally delivered service can be politically controversial; there are concerns about the cost and quality of privately delivered services; and many municipalities are heavily unionized workplaces, making the introduction of private services challenging. Finally, the private sector might not even be an option: in many remote or rural communities, there might not be the competition among private firms that is needed to create efficiency gains. In such circumstances, contracting or cooperating with another municipality is the only option for service delivery innovation.

In contrast to contractual arrangements, partnerships provide for a greater degree of integration. Contracts are in place for generally set – and relatively shorter – periods of time; partnerships focus on long-term integration and emphasize co-production, rather than contracted delivery. In this case, two (or more) municipalities form an arrangement to provide a service jointly – for example, to work together on the construction of an arena or a boundary road – with the municipalities involved bringing something to the partnership aside from need. Under purely contractual relationships, one (or more) partner has a need, perhaps based upon capacity or poor fiscal health, while the other has the ability to deliver the service. With a partnership, each brings something unique the table – perhaps one has policy expertise, while the other has a grant. A partnership, in effect, is the result of municipalities seeing enhanced value through cooperation. The project might be completed or delivered by one municipality alone, but it is improved by the inclusion of other members of the agreement.

Thus, "joint decision making and production" characterize partnerships (Klijn and Teisman 2000, 85–6). In these relationships, policy decision making and action can be fluid and changed. Partnerships are able to act and react, adjusting to changing circumstances and need. As such, there is a pooling of authority and autonomy (Huxman 1996; Sullivan and Skelcher 2002). Participating governments lose some of their ability to act independently in the policy area, ceding it to other local actors; ultimately, however, they benefit from tapping into the skill, expertise, or resources of partners.

Finally, municipalities might participate in networks, which can be seen as dynamic, yet informal, reciprocal groups of governmental actors. As Sullivan and Skelcher (2002, 5) tell us, networks are "constituted on the basis of informal relationships regulated by obligations of trust and reciprocity … [and] frequently grounded in individual relationships that transcend organizational boundaries and even organizational agendas." Networks are conceptualized as systems of actors (nodes) and relationships (ties) (Borgatti, Everett, and Johnson 2013; Kadushin 2012; Newman 2010; G. Robins 2015; Scott 2012). Actors are envisioned as separate entities, such as individuals within groups, departments within a municipality, or cities within a metropolitan area (LeRoux 2006; Wasserman and Faust 1994). Among these actors are ties that are conduits for the flow of material, such as funds or equipment, and non-material goods, such as information (Hanneman and Riddle 2005; LeRoux 2006). These ties are not mutually exclusive, meaning that networks can have multiple, overlapping relations.

Networks are fluid and can grow in response to a particular policy or service issue (Sullivan and Skelcher 2002). Such groupings also have an entrepreneurial aspect (Ayres and Davis 2000). Networks are generally conceived as being held together by values and trust gained through repeated interaction (Frederickson 1999; Thurmaier and Wood 2002). Their continuation, however, is not guaranteed: members can leave and enter, but within the network there is a cooperative spirit and a series of norms that promote trust and insulate the group from risk.

Much attention in this book is paid to formal contractual arrangements and partnerships that are formally codified. As mentioned above, there are research challenges involved in trying to sketch out informal relationships. Moreover, networked relationships are fairly well documented (see Borgatti, Everett, and Johnson 2013; Kadushin 2012; Newman 2010; G. Robins 2015; Scott 2012; Sullivan and Skelcher 2002). My aim is thus to provide synthesis and to shed new light on contractual and joint intermunicipal relationships in Canadian local government.

A Research Agenda for Interlocal Cooperation and Contracting in Canada

As discussed earlier, interlocal cooperation is an attractive concept to municipal decision makers. Whether a municipal administration is trying to lower costs or improve services, cooperation with another municipal government is usually discussed as an option. We should not, therefore, be surprised that municipalities of all shapes and sizes cooperate with one another.

In Canadian political science, intergovernmental relationships are an important area of study (see Bolleyer 2006; Cameron and Simeon 2002; Graefe, Simmons, and White 2013). This is, of course, for good reason, considering the history and development of the Canadian federation. This enthusiasm has not extended, however, to interlocal relationships. Much of the literature on intergovernmental relationships in Canada concerns vertical relationships, where municipalities have found a considerable home over the past ten years (see Graham and Andrew 2014; Horak 2013; Horak and Young 2012). Bilateral local relationships have received comparatively less scholarly attention.

There are some reasons this should be expected to change. First, as we will see in subsequent chapters, interlocal relationships exist across Canada in a variety of forms and states of success. Some of these relationships have existed for decades, others are new. Some are strong, others are fragile. Some are formal, others are informal. Some are still place, others have failed completely. These relationships deserve attention.

Second – and, again, I explore this fully in subsequent chapters – these interlocal relationships provide the framework for producing and delivering important – for many, vital – services such as fire and police protection, sanitation, water services and public transportation. Experimentation and innovation in servicing design thus should be encouraged. Interlocal cooperation provides an important forum for this, which is something we should embrace as a research community.

Finally, the study of interlocal cooperation and service sharing is important because it provides a better understanding of the alternatives in service delivery and institutional design. Improving governance should be the goal of any keen municipal practitioner. Privatization, institutional consolidation and innovations in service delivery are just a few options that could be examined. Collaborating with neighbouring governments ought to be included as well. To examine comparatively alternatives in service delivery, we need an accurate appraisal of our options. As Filipe Teles (2016, 8) argues in his book on interlocal cooperation in Europe, "one cannot claim to understand contemporary local governance if collaboration isn't included in its research agenda."

This book follows a similar line of thinking: interlocal cooperation is important and warrants academic enquiry. As such, I ask research questions across two main dimensions. First, assessing the cooperative:

- who is cooperating?
- what service and policy areas are involved?

Second, explaining the local cooperative process:

- why do municipalities cooperate?
- why do municipalities not cooperate?
- what leads to successful cooperative relationships?
- what leads to agreement failure?
- What roles do the provinces play in this process?

I answer these questions in several stages. In the second chapter, I review the state of interlocal cooperation and contracting in Canada by assessing the components of interlocal service agreements signed between 1995 and 2013 in twelve major Canadian metropolitan areas: Vancouver, Calgary, Edmonton, Saskatoon, Regina, Winnipeg, Toronto, Moncton, Ottawa, Saint John, St John's, and Thunder Bay. I also present a novel method of measuring the integration of individual agreements. Overall, I find that Canadian municipalities are cooperating at lower rates than US and European municipalities. Canadian municipalities are also forming fewer long-term agreements that integrate service or administrative functions, indicating that municipalities are preferring instead to form purpose-driven or policy-focused networks that address single service areas. For the most part, they are avoiding large-scale integration of administrative of policy areas.

In Chapter 3, I explain cooperation and detail the process of reaching agreement. I also address the relationship between private and public contracting, the motivation behind selecting certain partners, and the strategy behind approaching cooperative behaviour. On Chapter 4, I look at agreement failure and non-cooperation, explaining how municipalities cope with the breakdown of agreements. Chapter 5 explores the role of provincial governments in the cooperative process. As discussed above, the strength of provincial governments in governing local affairs is well known. At times, provincial governments have been major players in forcing cooperative activity upon municipalities; at other times, some provinces have dissuaded municipalities from forming certain cooperative relationships. Ultimately, the provinces can fill the gap if certain services agreements fail, meaning they can help to mitigate risk in this Canadian context. The final chapter presents conclusions and some further observations about the study of interlocal cooperation.

In each chapter, the research presented relies on primary documents – mostly in the form of interlocal agreements and government reports – interviews with local government practitioners, and two surveys concerning intermunicipal cooperation and contracting. The first survey examined was undertaken to determine the attitudes of local administrators and politicians towards the use of cooperation and interlocal agreements, and was distributed to municipal officials in Ontario between July and August 2015.[4] The survey received 707 responses from senior staff and politicians in small, medium, and large municipalities across the province, representing a 17 per cent response rate. The survey asked respondents to gauge their experience with past cooperative activity (if they had engaged in any) and rate their proclivity towards future cooperation under certain scenarios. The second survey was conducted in November 2012 by Ontario's Ministry of Municipal Affairs and Housing and was designed to assess the practice of interlocal cooperation in the province. The survey catalogued the number of interlocal agreements and the policy areas in which agreements had been signed, and examined various dimensions of the cooperative process, such as agreement failure. All 444 municipalities in the province were contacted by phone for the survey; 409 responded – a rate of 92.1 per cent. Respondents were either chief administrative officers or designated senior managers.[5]

The use of two surveys helps to close gaps in our understanding of interlocal cooperation among municipalities. Because municipalities in

Ontario have a reporting obligation to the provincial government, the high response rate to the 2012 survey helps to bolster the results of the relatively low response rate from the 2015 survey. Using two different surveys to examine a common practice can, however, create some challenges. The 2012 survey was designed and administered independently of the author; as such, there are a number of differences between the two surveys – for instance, in the way services are categorized. Also, the 2012 survey, administered by the ministry, does not delve as deeply into the motivations of those considering interlocal cooperation or contracting as a service delivery model. As such, it is difficult to align the surveys and combine certain questions. As a result, results from each survey are often presented throughout the book independently of each other and used where the focus of the survey can add value to the discussion at hand.

Both surveys contain responses only from Ontario. This, of course, does not account for variations in attitudes towards interlocal cooperation and contracting throughout the country. I do not rely on evidence from these surveys alone, however, but couple them with an empirical examination of 648 interlocal agreements from municipalities across Canada. Throughout the book, I also present the results of primary interviews conducted with administrators to get an in-depth perspective on interlocal contracting and cooperation in the hope of providing a holistic perspective on the practice.

2 Mapping the Cooperative Landscape

One of the main objectives of the research for this book was to find out which municipalities are cooperating and contracting with others and which services or policy areas are involved. In this chapter, I present survey evidence collected by the Ontario Ministry of Municipal Affairs and Housing in 2012, along with analysis of over 600 interlocal agreements from across Canada. Using the two data sources provided a unique perspective on the state of intermunicipal cooperation and contracting in Canada, allowing the researcher to obtain information about the perception of shared services, while diving deeper into the actual agreements themselves – exploring not only the policy areas and timelines in which they were signed, but also the various components of the agreements, permitting a view into the context of each arrangement.

The Ontario survey, which examined the level of interlocal cooperation in that province, did not probe the feelings of respondents towards the cooperative process, but it provides a robust sketch of the state of cooperation across the province and some basic insight into the motivations and satisfaction of those involved in completing these agreements. Of the 409 municipalities that responded to the province's survey (Ontario had 444 municipalities at the time of the survey), 378 (92.4 per cent) indicated that they shared or contracted services of some kind with another municipality; only 31 (7.6 per cent) did not cooperate formally with other municipalities. Of those that cooperated, 331 reported having one or more formal agreements, while 32 reported having some kind of informal arrangement – an agreement not written down or legally codified.

Respondents with interlocal agreements were asked to indicate which policy areas were involved (Figure 2.1). Most of the agreements concern emergency services and roads maintenance. The review below of shared services and contractual agreements from twelve Census Metropolitan Areas (CMAs) across the county shows similar results. Many

Figure 2.1. Interlocal Agreements by Policy Area

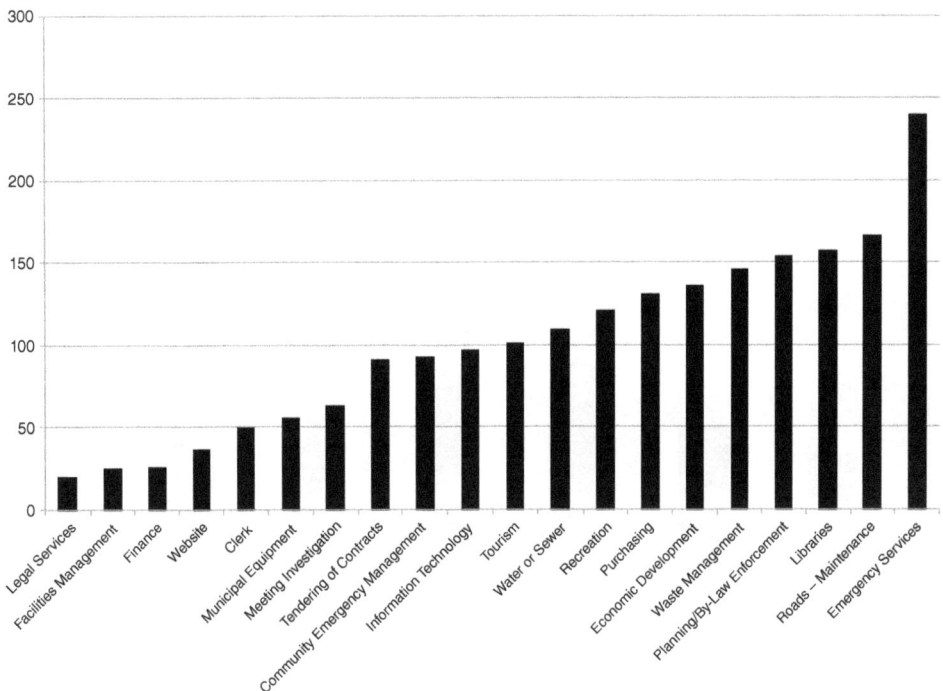

Source: Author's compilation.

of these emergency services agreements involve mutual aid, which essentially authorizes the municipalities to respond to emergencies in the other partners to the agreement. Most of these are in place for insurance purposes, while also ensuring adequate coverage across a particular jurisdiction in the event of a fire.

Figure 2.2 demonstrates the type of resources involved, as described by survey respondents. Of those municipalities sharing or contracting services, cost is the most frequent resource exchanged, although some do involve the sharing or exchange of staff, equipment, and facilities. For the most part, however, financial resources are changing hands in these arrangements.

To complement the survey data from the Ontario Ministry of Municipal Affairs and Housing, interlocal agreements were collected in twelve major Canadian metropolitan areas: Vancouver, Calgary, Edmonton, Saskatoon, Regina, Winnipeg, Toronto, Moncton, Saint John,

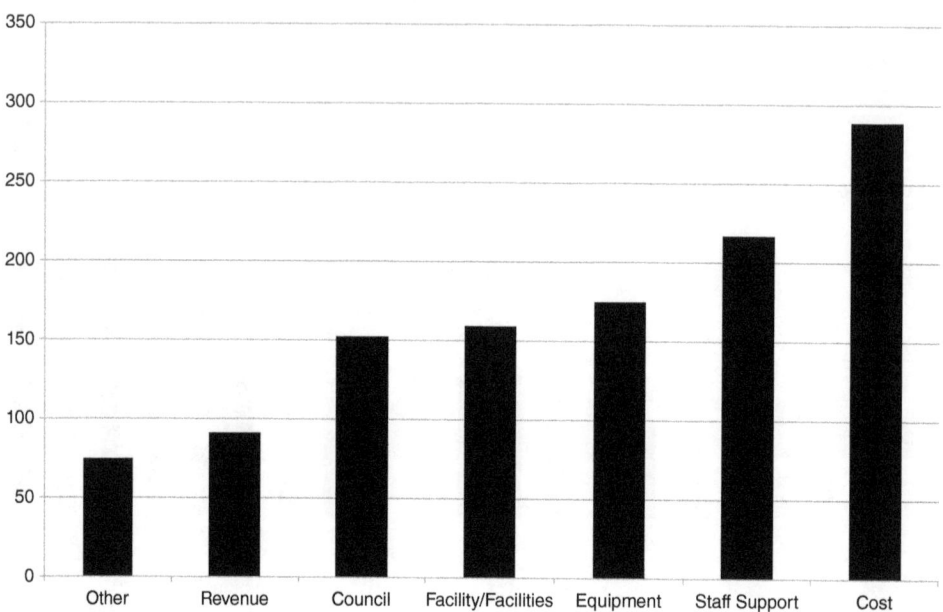

Figure 2.2. Local Resources Shared

Source: Author's compilation.

St John's, Thunder Bay, and Ottawa-Gatineau; Montreal was excluded for reasons explained later in the chapter. The ministry survey did not include the actual agreements, making it difficult to categorize them beyond policy area and type of resources exchanged. The individual components of the agreements also tell a story about the nature of the relationships. For instance, to what degree do these agreements bind participants? What sort of legal protections are in place? There is a growing strain in literature on this topic demonstrating that the components of these agreements provide a view into how each participant views trust, risk, and the prospects of coordination (see Feiock 2013; Nelles and Alcantara 2011; Post 2004). An agreement with more legal protection, for instance, could indicate a lack of trust or a degree of unfamiliarity between participants. As such, examining individual agreements gives researchers a degree of nuance that survey data cannot.

Before analysing the individual agreements, it is important to discuss the data-collection process. When looking for interlocal agreements, it is challenging to determine where to limit the collection area. For example, there is no strict agreement on which communities fall into the Greater Toronto Area. While it is understood that Toronto is part of the metropolitan area, what about large regional centres such as Hamilton? What, perhaps, of cities that are some distance from Toronto, but are still within the city's economic, cultural, or social influence, such as Guelph, Waterloo, Kitchener, Cambridge, or even London? Thus, to avoid any such complications, I used the CMA boundaries as determined by Statistics Canada to limit the study areas. CMAs provide an area broad enough to capture a variety of interlocal activity because of geographic proximity, but not too large to dilute the findings and leave the study area open for significant debate. This choice, however, limits the number of CMAs that could be analysed. For instance, the amalgamation of the Halifax Regional Municipality in 1996 means that the Halifax CMA contains only one municipality, Halifax, making interlocal activity impossible.

The CMAs in the study provide a great deal of variety. They include Canada's largest city-regions (Vancouver, Toronto), fastest-growing city-regions (Calgary, Edmonton), Prairie cities (Saskatoon, Regina), Atlantic cities (Saint John, St John's), one that has undergone a significant degree of restructuring (Winnipeg), one that crosses provincial borders (Ottawa-Gatineau), and small to mid-sized centres (Moncton, Thunder Bay). The sample thus allows for the inclusion of urban centres, mid-sized communities, and even remote municipal regions in the study. As such, one can account for a variety of factors that might influence interlocal cooperation and service sharing.

Table 2.1 lists the population and number of governments included in each CMA.[1] A full listing of the municipalities in each CMA is provided in the Appendix.

There is a large variation in size between the CMAs selected. Toronto is by far the largest, which should come as no surprise. Thunder Bay, Saint John, and Moncton are the smallest. The variation in the number of governing units within each CMA is significant. Some, such as Calgary, have only a handful of governments (8), while others, such as Edmonton, have as many as 31 municipalities, which in turn also allows us to examine the impact of group size. In total, however, the twelve chosen CMAs are the country's largest and have a combined population of close to 15 million, a sizeable portion of the Canadian total. As such, the sample should provide a good understanding of the dynamics of intermunicipal cooperation in Canada.

Interlocal Agreements in Canada

In total, 648 agreements signed between 1995 and 2013 were found in the selected CMAs.[2] This period was chosen for a number of reasons, chiefly because it is long enough to account for major provincial

Table 2.1. Census Metropolitan Areas Chosen for the Study

Census Metropolitan Area	Population	Number of Governing Units
Vancouver	2,504,300	22
Calgary	1,439,800	8
Edmonton	1,363,300	31
Saskatoon	305,000	23
Regina	241,400	17
Winnipeg	793,400	11
Toronto	6,129,900	23
Moncton	144,770	14
Ottawa	1,323,783	15
Saint John	126,202	18
St John's	205,955	12
Thunder Bay	121,621	7

Source: Author's compilation.

initiatives – such as amalgamation and various rounds of policy downloading[3] – but recent enough that many of these agreements are still relevant and active. At the same time, the sample goes back only as far as 1995 because municipalities have some difficulty securing documents prior to that date. Only formal agreements are included. Although municipalities also engage in informal agreements – agreements that are understood to municipal policy makers but not officially codified – this practice is hard to account for and understand, mainly because of the absence of documentation. It is challenging to understand the full scope of the informal arrangement for someone outside the organization.[4] As such, it was determined prudent to study only formal agreements.

There is a great deal of variation in the number of agreements among the CMAs, as displayed in Table 2.2. The most obvious is the disparity among Toronto, Edmonton, and Ottawa, which have many more agreements than the other CMAs. The high numbers in Toronto and Edmonton might be easier to account for: Toronto is Canada's most populated metropolitan area, and it is understandable that officials in this CMA might rely more heavily on interlocal cooperation and contracting to provide policy and service continuity to such an expansive and growing region.[5] Edmonton, on the other hand, has the highest number of governing units, 31, within its CMA. It also has the largest land area of the CMAs under study. Both of these factors might have led to the creation of more interlocal agreements, and, similar to Toronto, Edmonton is a large and growing region.

Ottawa presents a different story. Although the Ottawa region is certainly growing, its growth rate is not near that of Toronto or Edmonton.

Table 2.2. Interlocal Agreements per Census Metropolitan Area

Census Metropolitan Area	Number of Agreements
Vancouver	56
Calgary	30
Edmonton	153
Saskatoon	11
Regina	13
Winnipeg	15
Toronto	132
Moncton	23
Ottawa	149
Saint John	17
St John's	23
Thunder Bay	26

Source: Author's compilation.

Ottawa itself went through a large amalgamation in 2001 that saw the former Regional Municipality of Ottawa-Carleton consolidated into a single government[6], which certainly reduces the amount of potential cooperation, given the large land area of the municipality in comparison to its surrounding area. The Ottawa CMA as defined by Statistics Canada (officially referred to as the Ottawa-Gatineau CMA) spans the Ontario-Quebec border, mostly capturing municipalities on the Quebec side. This has had an effect on the number of interlocal agreements in the area: only 20 of the 149 total agreements in the Ottawa CMA have been signed in Ontario, indicating that the majority of interlocal contracting for the region is occurring on the Quebec side of the border.

There are some explanations for the differences in agreement formation between the Ontario and Quebec sides of the Ottawa CMA. The first is that twelve of the fifteen municipalities in the CMA are in Quebec. This means they have more potential partners. On the Ontario side, Ottawa's amalgamation significantly reduced the number of potential partners, leaving only Russell and Clarence-Rockland outside the CMA; moreover, the urbanized parts of these municipalities are some distance from Ottawa, making interlocal cooperation or contracting an unnatural fit for many types of services. As well, despite their close proximity, there are no interlocal agreements in place between Ontario and Quebec municipalities within the CMA, leaving Ottawa with fewer potential partners if it chooses not to explore partnerships with municipalities in Quebec. Of note as well is that many of the agreements on the Quebec side are short-term, terminal agreements that, if renegotiated, will result in the formation of a new agreement. For example, the municipalities of Denholm and Bowman, Quebec, have a series of road maintenance agreements that end and are renegotiated every year (or in some cases two years). In total, the two municipalities have eight agreements covering the same subject. While this is a perfectly defensible practice, a more typical format is to have one agreement that is reviewed periodically and can be renewed if not terminated. From a methodological standpoint, such an agreement would result in one agreement, as opposed to the eight signed between Denholm and Bowman. The strategy seen in the agreements signed between Denholm and Bowman, however, appears to be common in Quebec, likely stemming from a unique organizational culture in local administration in that province.

Over time, there has been a general increase in the number of agreements signed, as Figure 2.3 demonstrates; the increase, however, has not been consistent. As well, relatively few actors are involved: the average number of participants for each agreement is 2.86, suggesting that most municipalities prefer to form agreements with a small number of partners – indeed, the vast majority of the agreements are bilateral. For the most part, municipalities are shying away from forming multilateral agreements, which is consistent with past research on cooperation that finds that smaller policy networks are easier to manage and direct (Post 2004). Achieving consensus among fewer actors is much easier than within a larger group. Additionally, the transaction costs inherent with signing intermunicipal agreements are lower in groups with fewer participants. An interesting finding is that many of these agreements are being formed on the periphery of the CMAs studied: roughly half of the agreements do not include the central city in the CMA.

Figure 2.4 displays the policy areas of the agreements collected from the CMAs included in this study.[7] The majority concern emergency services, which is consistent with US literature on interlocal cooperation (Andrew 2008). Most of the emergency services agreements involve fire protection, chiefly in the form of mutual-aid or fee-for-service agreements.

Given the importance of emergency services, it should be not be too surprising that these are the most commonly shared or contracted service by municipalities in the sample. Here, geographic coverage is vital in maintaining public safety. No municipal politician or administrator wants to see community members harmed, and residents expect that, in the event of a fire or flood, there will be an adequate response from emergency officials. Beyond this basic rationale, municipalities are often compelled under provincial mandate to supply emergency services consistently throughout their jurisdiction. Partnering or contracting with another municipality can help achieve this legislative goal.

Figure 2.3. Interlocal Agreements, 1995–2013

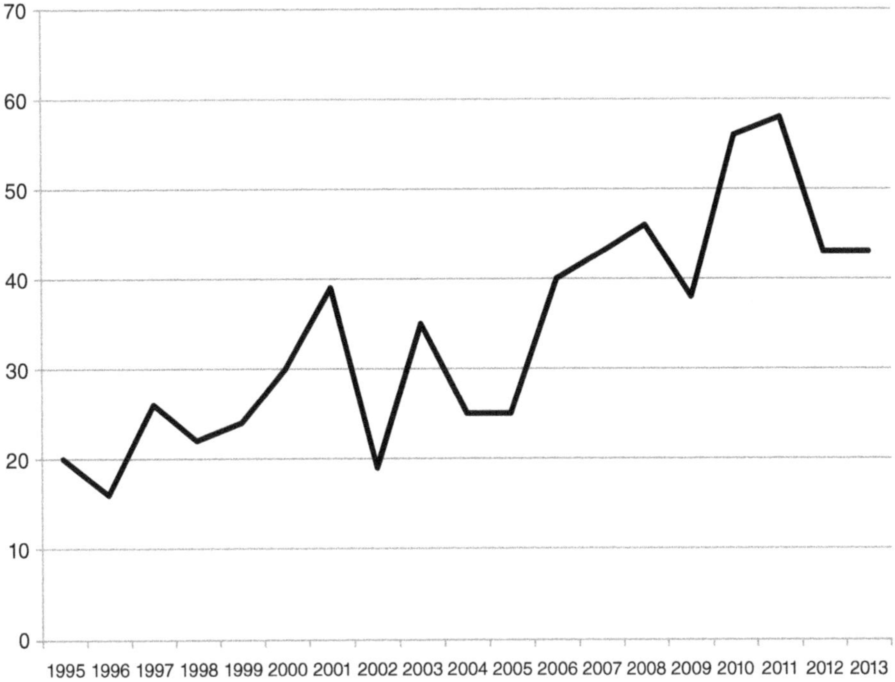

Source: Author's compilation.

Emergency services agreements tend to come in one of three forms. The first is a mutual-aid agreement. In such an arrangement, two or more municipalities sign an agreement that ensures that emergency services personnel from one community respond to an emergency in the other if called upon (Spicer 2014). For instance, if a fire occurs close to the border of two communities that have a mutual-aid agreement, both fire services respond. If the neighbouring fire service is closer to the fire or better equipped to respond, the agreement provides for communication with the other community's fire service, indemnity for its response, and, in some cases, compensation for the use of the resources. These types of arrangements are fairly common, as they are relatively costless and ensure adequate jurisdictional coverage in the event of an emergency. The agreements are in effect only under certain circumstances – namely, an emergency – so there are no ongoing costs to operate or monitor the arrangement.

Figure 2.4. Policy Areas of Interlocal Agreements in the Study

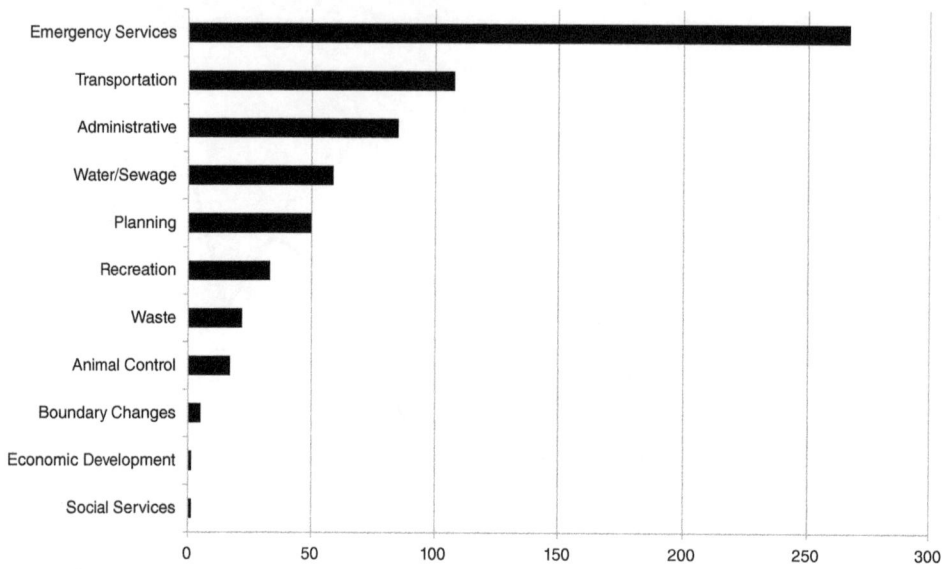

Source: Author's compilation.

The other two forms of emergency services agreements should by now be familiar to readers: service sharing and contracting. Emergency services is a multifaceted policy space, which allows for certain service areas to be parsed and shared or contracted, which again adds to its popularity. Municipalities need not share or contract the entirety of their fire services or emergency response, but instead share or contract one component of it. For instance, two or more municipalities can share the administration costs of their fire services, but keep their fire services separate and independent of each other.

For example, the Towns of Midland and Penetanguishene, Ontario, instead of hiring two chiefs to run their independent fire services, share a fire chief, splitting the cost of the chief's $115,000 annual salary, as well as the $47,793 salary of the chief's executive assistant (Dunning 2015). Approximately 60 members of the two fire departments remained at their own stations, while the chief's time is split between the two locations (Dunning 2015). In total, the two municipalities estimated that sharing the cost of one chief was then saving them approximately $140,000 a year (Dunning 2015). After two years of operations, however, it was determined that the agreement managed to produce only about $12,000 in savings, although the chief argued that further savings had materialized by avoiding possible tax increases (Mendler 2017).[8]

As noted, the emergency services portfolio is complex, and municipalities might want to contract with another municipality to provide certain kinds of these services – for instance, emergency communications or the use of specialized equipment such as air support or tools for certain types of rescue operations. Municipalities also might wish to contract fire services or police protection for a certain area of their jurisdiction to an adjacent municipality that has closer facilities it can deploy, thus avoiding the construction of a new fire or police station. For example, the City of Leduc and Leduc County, Alberta, have a history of engaging in such forms of contracting for service or geographic-specific elements of emergency management (Leduc County 2017).

Agreements also may be comprehensive. One such is the Southern Alberta Emergency Management Resource Sharing Agreement, struck in 2007, which establishes a broad framework for service sharing and contracting for eight jurisdictions in southern Alberta: the City of Medicine Hat, the Town of Pincher Creek, the Town of Willow Creek, the Town of Taber, Vulcan County, the Town of Coalhurst, the City of Lethbridge, and Lethbridge County. The agreement establishes a protocol for emergency response, sets out a fee schedule for cost recovery after emergency response across boundaries, and covers delegation of authority, a threshold for activation, and a formalized resource request. Most important, the agreement addresses the role of each municipality's emergency services personnel to respond to an emergency and provides indemnity in the case of a response. The agreement thus contains both sharing and contracting elements to ensure adequate emergency services coverage over a large region.

A particular aspect of shared or municipally contracted emergency services agreements is the desire to assist other municipalities in times of need. There is a certain altruism that is virtually absent of other service-sharing areas – an incentive and motivation structure that I discuss at greater length later in the book. The debate in Lethbridge on whether to join the Southern Alberta Emergency Management Resource Sharing Agreement illustrates this process. During the debate, Lethbridge councillor Joe Mauro asked staff why the agreement was structured on cost recovery rather than on profit making (Fominoff 2018). Lethbridge had more resources and capacity in its emergency services department than many of the other signatories to the agreement, and could very well have established interlocal service agreements on a profit-making model. Deputy Fire Chief Dana Terry argued, however, that this should not be the City's central motivation:

When another community is in a time of need, should we be making money on that? We do want to get our costs back, because it does cost us to send people and responders out. But the whole idea is that we want to help the communities and not place an additional burden on them that may not be necessary. We want to help our neighbours. We've called on them to help us as well. So we recognize the need for it and we recognize the importance of calling for help when we need it and getting it when we need it. And then on our part, to be there as a good neighbour as well. (Fominoff 2018)

Lethbridge eventually signed on to the agreement on a cost-recovery basis, but the debate illustrates the views of certain municipal actors when it comes to sharing or contracting emergency services, which they consider a matter of one municipality assisting another, which runs counter to charging another community to turn a profit.

Altruism, however, might go only so far in shared services. In February 2015, a fire broke out on the Makwa Sahgaiehcan First Nation reserve in Saskatchewan, which unfortunately claimed the lives of two young Indigenous children (Capiral 2015). Compounding the family's and community's grief was the fact that the Village of Loon Lake had terminated a long-standing agreement to provide fire protection for the reserve just three weeks earlier, citing an unpaid debt by the band council of $3,300 for previous emergency deployments (Capiral 2015). As a result, since the First Nation community did not have its own fire service, there was no emergency response once the fire started.

Under the original agreement, the band had agreed to pay an annual $5,000 fee plus the costs for each fire the Loon Lake fire department attended. On 2 October 2012, the then chief of the band government, Richard Ben, wrote a letter to the Village administration cancelling the contract and insisting that the payment model be altered so that, instead of paying an annual fee, the band would simply pay for the cost to fight each fire (Capiral 2015). The Village agreed, and in January 2013 a new agreement was completed that called on the band government to pay $400 an hour for use of a fire truck, $300 an hour for a water truck, and $25 an hour for each fire fighter attending to a fire on the reserve (Capiral 2015).

In terminating the agreement, Village administrators argued that the band government had stopped paying its bills in 2014 and had not responded to any correspondence regarding the outstanding amounts owned to Loon Lake. The administrators said they had sent notice of termination to the reserve in January 2015 (Capiral 2015). For their part, the band administrators in Makwa Sahgaiehcan argued that they were unaware that the contract had been cancelled and were under the impression that the Loon Lake fire department would still be responding to calls on reserve (Capiral 2015).

The majority of agreements in the transportation category are public transit agreements, such as those signed between Edmonton and its neighbouring municipalities. The next most frequent area of cooperation is administrative services, which includes all items relating to staffing and other matters of corporate services, such as information technology and data sharing. A growing trend in interlocal cooperation is the sharing of staff and administrative resources, including legal services.

Agreements between municipalities can be categorized generally as either adaptive or restrictive. The two types create very different policy outcomes, and provide clues as to the nature of the relationship between the parties prior to the signing of an agreement. An agreement is "restrictive" if it is based upon and closely adheres to a specific set of rules, generally rooted in provincial law and local ordinances (Andrew 2008). These types of agreements provide very little room for interpretation, and are challenging to alter because they tend to have fixed expiration dates and clear procedures for termination. While lacking flexibility, restrictive agreements do provide stability over the life of an agreement, as both sides know what is expected of them financially and administratively, along with full knowledge of the penalties involved in breaking or deviating from the terms of the agreement. Examples of restrictive agreements include contracts – such as service agreements – and lease agreements.

"Adaptive" agreements, in contrast, are more open and provide more generalized guidelines for local coordination efforts. Simon Andrew (2008, 10) argues that adaptive agreements are "purposely designed to complement pre-existing policies as opposed to a neatly crafted joint vision to improve the overall welfare of the participating local governments' constituents." What adaptive agreements lack in stability, they make up in flexibility, as they usually do not include strict financial or administrative outlines and are more easily altered if the partners deem it necessary. Adaptive agreements also tend to lack some of the safeguards traditionally found in restrictive agreements, such as termination clauses and expiration dates. Examples of adaptive agreements include mutual-aid agreements, memoranda of understanding, letters of agreement, and informal arrangements.

Restrictive agreements tend to be used in policy areas that have large budgets or for services not already provided by a municipality (Post 2004; Stein 1990). Examples include water or sewer servicing and the construction of new capital projects such as recreation centres or long-term care facilities. In such areas, restrictive agreements are preferred since adaptive agreements can result in one partner's not fulfilling its financial or administrative responsibilities, thereby creating service gaps for residents.

Adaptive agreements are generally used to complement existing services, such as mutual-aid agreements for fire, or where service gaps would not create financial hardship, such as road maintenance or snow removal. In such cases, each municipality has the administrative infrastructure necessary to provide the service independently, but uses an adaptive service agreement to provide an additional layer of security or to allow the municipality to cut costs (Lynn 2005). Some additional examples of adaptive agreement policy areas include staff training, library services, and cultural services.

Adaptive agreements, however, also come with a degree of risk – namely, a high level of behavioural uncertainty, which occurs when a supplier municipality is tempted to capture a larger share of the aggregate gains (Shrestha 2010). This risk is largely absent from restrictive agreements, but adaptive agreements are nearly always at risk of being renegotiated or reneged upon. That is not to say, however, that restrictive agreements are without risk, since general environmental uncertainties, such as the unexpected breakdown of technology or sudden occurrences of natural incidents affecting supply, are possibilities for all types of agreements (Shrestha 2010).

As Table 2.3 shows, the vast majority of the agreements – approximately 88 per cent – are restrictive, and most – 79 per cent – also include termination clauses that allow at least one partner to leave the arrangement. These clauses may include procedures and timelines for withdrawal, such as the requirement to submit a termination notice in writing within sixty days of the proposed withdrawal. Procedures and timing vary by agreement, however, with 58 per cent containing expiry clauses stating that the agreement will terminate automatically after a set period unless the jurisdictions included in the agreement want to extend it.

Although most jurisdictions prefer agreements with termination and expiry clauses, very few include clauses for monitoring, such as the creation of joint boards or commissions (5 per cent) or dispute-resolution mechanisms (13 per cent). The high rates of termination clauses could indicate that many communities view their ability to terminate the agreement as a form of dispute resolution; consequently, each signatory's ability to leave the agreement at any time is, in itself, an incentive to seek an informal resolution to any impasse.

The prevalence of expiry and termination clauses also indicates that most jurisdictions prefer to establish agreements that carry a low level of risk. Although these agreements are formalized, they are for set durations and allow either partner to leave the agreement if it feels that

Table 2.3. Components of Interlocal Agreements in the Study

Component	Number of Agreements	Share (%)
Expiry clauses	378	58
Termination clauses	515	79
Creation of joint committees or boards	34	5
Dispute-resolution mechanisms	84	13
Total restrictive agreements	569	88
Total adaptive agreements	79	12

Source: Author's compilation.

participating is no longer in its best interest. Including termination clauses also prevents future councils from being bound to the decisions of past councils by not committing them to contracts that could limit available political and fiscal choices. Only a minority of agreements established independent authorities to monitor and execute the content of the agreement, with a similar number having built-in dispute-resolution mechanisms. This indicates that municipalities are creating agreements to establish policy-specific and purpose-driven networks of cooperation, rather than long-term relationships.

The vast majority of agreements are restrictive, in that they contain formal legal procedures that bind each participant to its actions. As previously discussed, these types of agreements aim to mitigate risk and ensure that expectations for each partner are well known. Adaptive agreements are mainly used for mutual aid and protection, which is consistent with past literature on emergency response agreements (Andrew 2009). In both areas, municipalities largely use cooperative agreements to supplement existing services, which – not coincidentally – are the types of situations that call for adaptive agreements. These agreements are formed largely to add to existing services and to ensure continuity. Although two municipalities already might have a fire department, a mutual-aid agreement could provide additional protection to potentially underserviced border regions. The municipalities in the CMAs under study use adaptive agreements in policy areas similar to those of US municipalities, although provincial regulation might be forcing them to use restrictive agreements more often than they would otherwise.

Some initial conclusions can be drawn from this scan of the 648 agreements collected (see Table 2.4). The first is that Canadian municipalities do not cooperate as much as one might expect. Considering the size of the CMAs selected, finding only 648 agreements over a nearly twenty-year

Table 2.4. Types of Interlocal Agreements, by Census Metropolitan Area

Census Metropolitan Area	Type of Agreement		
	Contract	Memorandum of Understanding	Mutual Aid
Vancouver	48	3	5
Toronto	113	7	12
Winnipeg	8	6	1
Saskatoon	10	0	1
Regina	9	4	0
Edmonton	135	10	8
Calgary	27	3	0
Moncton	16	1	6
Ottawa	149	0	0
Saint John	16	0	1
St John's	17	6	0
Thunder Bay	26	0	0
Total	574	40	34

Source: Author's compilation.

time span was surprising, especially given the number of agreements found in other countries using similar collection methods (see Andrew 2008; LeRoux and Carr 2007). Most agreements were found in Toronto, Edmonton, and Ottawa. As discussed, the Toronto and Edmonton CMAs are large, growing regions with many municipalities, providing ample chance and reason to seek out cooperative and contractual arrangements with other local governments. In Ottawa, the cross-border nature of the CMA has created a unique pattern of agreement formation, which has increased the overall number of agreements. Aside from these three, most of the CMAs selected – regardless of size or location – have formed very few interlocal agreements. Of the signed agreements, most involve emergency services such as mutual aid or emergency communications arrangements. Most are contracts and, therefore, classified as "restrictive," meaning that they come with a great deal of legal protection. Later in this chapter, I examine the "intensity" of these agreements in order to get a better sense of how they are (or are not) being used to bind municipalities together.

Methodological Challenges

Intermunicipal cooperation is a practice that some observers might find difficult to understand. Few municipalities publicize or make interlocal agreements accessible. For the most part, these agreements are considered to be internal administrative matters, rather than something that ought to concern the general public. As such, anyone wishing to examine any agreements their municipality has in place usually must ask municipal staff for permission or (as a worst-case scenario) submit a Freedom of Information Act request to secure them. Moreover, some agreements are not formalized, meaning there is no documentation or paper trail to support the service or policy areas, making tracing the agreement and examining its contents impossible. This brief section addresses both of these challenges and how they relate to documenting the impact of interlocal cooperation in Canada.

Interlocal agreements are public documents, but they are not always available to the public. Very few agreements are available online. For the most part, the agreements analysed in this project needed to be requested or gained through Freedom of Information Act requests.[9] Viewing these agreements or securing copies was challenging to do for this particular project, but it is certainly not the first to encounter such difficulties. Sancton, James, and Ramsay (2000) had serious challenges trying to examine intermunicipal agreements for a study comparing various modes of local service delivery, and found there was limited documentation and internal knowledge surrounding such arrangements. Generally, only one person within the organization had any understanding of the mechanics of each agreement. Additionally, very little formal documentation of any agreements existed, and where it did, documentation was difficult to access. Sancton, James, and Ramsay also found a lack of administrative control and a complete absence of any type of evaluation system, leading them to conclude that much more accountability and transparency was needed around the interlocal agreement process, especially when compared to other models of service delivery and governance (2000, 64).[10]

Most interlocal agreements are written legal documents – they are formalized and have legal protection. The partners agree to the terms of the arrangement and legally codify the document, which includes legal sanctions. Most municipalities opt for such arrangements, as they help to reduce risk. Informal arrangements, however, are unwritten, flexible, and open – qualities that are attractive to certain municipal practitioners – but they do not contain the same types of protections as formal agreements. The execution of an informal arrangement is usually the responsibility of a small group of administrators who understand its terms.

The challenge for the researcher, first, is simply discovering the existence of these agreements. Not only are there no written records, but many local government practitioners might not be entirely aware of them or their contents. Second, the agreements cannot be shared or measured, and their components cannot be analysed. As a result, the arrangements cannot be compared, creating significant hurdles for evaluating their use and effectiveness. Such challenges are the reason other studies examining interlocal cooperation in Canada have focused only on formal, written agreements (see LeSage Jr., McMillan, and Hepburn 2008; Sancton, James, and Ramsay 2000; Spicer 2014), and this study, for the same reasons, also looks solely at formal agreements.

The agreements collected represent the best efforts of the author to be as comprehensive as possible. Throughout the data-collection process, many municipalities did not respond to requests for documentation. To complete the document collection for this project, 76 separate Access to Information requests had to be filed. In some cases, municipalities ignored these requests, and further requests were required. The average number of days for completion of the request for agreements was 118. Another major challenge was verifying the accuracy of the number of agreements. In some cases, requests had to be made to individual departments to ensure an accurate count of agreements from each municipality. Such problems highlight persistent accountability issues with interlocal servicing – namely, a low level of transparency and a lack of internal understanding of existing servicing relationships.

Persistent efforts were not sufficient to obtain documents from every municipality in the sample. In the Toronto CMA, the municipalities of Halton Hills, Milton, and Markham did not provide agreements, despite a number of requests, including under the Freedom of Information Act. Ultimately, municipalities are under no obligation to grant these requests, but given that these are public documents, it would be in the interest of accountability and transparency to provide them.

No region in Canada demonstrates the challenges of transparency in interlocal servicing more than the municipalities in the Montreal CMA. For more than a year, attempts were made in vain to obtain the interlocal agreements of every municipality in the CMA. Of the 89 municipalities in the CMA, only 25 responded to requests for documentation. Four of these municipalities – Châteauguay, Saint-Bruno-de-Montarville, Chambly, and Candiac – indicated that they did not have any agreements. Further research indicated that Châteauguay and Chambly did in fact have agreements with other municipalities, which were provided by other administrations. Two municipalities outright refused to provide copies of their agreement, even after the completion of Freedom of Information Act requests.

Although agreements from the majority of municipalities within the Montreal CMA could not be secured, 211 agreements were collected, indicating that the Montreal CMA has a fairly cooperative ethos. It is a shame that this could not be confirmed by exploring agreements from the entire region, although some consistencies with the other CMAs were found. For example, most of the agreements collected – 122, or roughly 58 per cent – concerned emergency services.[11] Unfortunately, however, there was insufficient information on the Montreal CMA to include it in the analysis in this book.

Agreement Intensity and the Nature of Local Partnership

Purely descriptive measures tell us only half the story when it comes to interlocal cooperation and contracting. How committed are these communities to partnership? To better understand this aspect of the regional story, I employ an index to measure "cooperative intensity." The concept of "cooperative intensity" was introduced to gain a more comprehensive understanding of the types of agreements being reached among municipalities (Nelles and Alcantara 2011). Simply put, not all agreements are created equal. Some result in greater integration than others, which makes relying on descriptive measures alone problematic. Context, in such analysis, can be, and often is, lost. Cooperative intensity, by comparison, was introduced as a measure of the strength of commitment of the parties to a partnership (Nelles 2009; Perkmann 2003). As a tool of measurement, cooperative intensity is the degree of authority and resources sacrificed by each party to collective control in the interest in long-term integration (Nelles and Alcantara 2011). As an example, an agreement that results in the formation of a joint planning body would be seen as more intense than a non-binding mutual-aid agreement that does not result in a pooling of authority and policy autonomy. Basic servicing agreements, then, are differentiated from those agreements that produce significantly more complex cooperative arrangements.

The most comprehensive Canadian study using institutional integration measures is Nelles and Alcantara's 2011 examination of intergovernmental relations between municipal and Indigenous governments in British Columbia. Nelles and Alcantara use three different measures: timing, binding, and institutional integration. "Timing" refers to the formal duration of the partnership. Agreements that have limited time frames have lower intensities than those left open-ended. As Nelles and Alcantara describe, limited agreements are considered less intense than indefinite agreements because a negotiated duration builds in guaranteed renegotiation points. Limited partnerships, therefore, have "escape routes" that can end partnerships.

The second measure introduced by Nelles and Alcantara (2011) is referred to as "binding." Agreements that are legally binding are considered more intense than non-binding agreements. In this measure, however, there is also a gradation of intensity, whereas agreements that are not legally binding, but outline dispute-resolution processes, are indicative of an intermediate level of commitment to the partnership.

The final element is "institutional integration," which refers to the distance that participating actors have from day-to-day decision making of the partnership. Where actors retain control of decision making, there is more control over outcomes than if the parties agree to let professional managers and non-governmental actors take the lead in managing collective interests. Nelles and Alcantara (2011) classify these types of arrangements from low-intensity institutional arrangements, such as simple contracting agreements, to high-intensity, such as joint or third-party governing bodies.

Although the concept of cooperative intensity helps to differentiate between agreements and provides context to the types of institutional arrangements that local actors construct, the dimensions of fiscal intensity and policy intensity have been added to further assist in classifying interlocal agreements. Fiscal intensity refers to the level of fiscal integration and insulation from partnerships, while policy intensity helps to classify the policy context of each relationship.

Fiscal intensity has two main components: exchange and risk. Exchange refers to the amount of financial resources allocated to the agreement. Many agreements are formed with no cost attached (for example, memoranda of understanding or communications agreements) or involve only the exchange of resources when certain conditions are met (for example, mutual-aid agreements, whereby costs are recovered in the event of an emergency response). Such agreements would be considered low intensity. Other agreements that involve consistent payment for goods or services (such as contractual servicing agreements) would be considered higher intensity, while agreements that involve the long-term integration of resources would be placed even higher on the scale of intensity.

The second measure of fiscal intensity is referred to as risk. The degree to which actors insulate themselves from integration matters in determining the overall strength of the partnership. Agreements that expose actors to risk are considered to have a higher measure of agreement intensity than those that do not – in other words, agreements that leave fewer checks and safeguards indicate that partners have greater faith in the institutional composition of the agreement and the overall outcome of the partnership. Agreements that come with a high degree of financial integration and risk mitigation indicate that the partners have lower levels of confidence about long-term cooperation.

The final measure is policy intensity. As mentioned earlier, not all agreements are created equal. This is also true when it comes to examining the policy areas of each cooperative agreement. Policy intensity is intended to measure the relative importance and necessity of provision of the policy areas under partnership. Certain policy areas, such as emergency services, are considered much more necessary to a municipality than others.[12] Cooperation in these areas might be easier to achieve because of the relative importance of provision. Other areas of municipal servicing, such as library or recreation services, are considered desirable, but not necessary for the functioning of a municipality. Policy intensity differentiates between these policy areas by identifying and measuring mandatory policy areas (such as emergency services), necessary policy areas (such as transportation or planning), and optional policy areas (such as recreation).[13]

Each agreement component is provided with a metric that places it on a spectrum of cooperative action that runs from 0 to 1. Intensity scores closely follow the original work by Nelles and Alcantara (2011). Scores were assigned by evaluating the text of each document. Each component was converted into a metric so that the agreement could be placed along the spectrum. In terms of cooperative intensity, scores were assigned based on the timing, binding, and integration of each agreement. For timing, a value of 0 was assigned if the term of the agreement was limited and 1 if left unspecified. Degree of legal binding was assessed using a value of 0 for non-binding agreements, 0.5 for agreements with dispute-resolution mechanisms, and 1 for agreements that contained termination clauses or were otherwise stated to be legally binding. Finally, values from 1 to 7 were assessed based on the strongest institutional form of the agreement. Simple service contracts or communication agreements were assigned a value of 1; other institutional forms were assessed as follows: collaboration (2), unspecified timing of meetings (3), regular meetings (base value of 4, with a decimal value for number of meetings committed to in the document – for instance, biannual meetings would net an institutionalization score of 4.2), collaborative implementation (5), and creation of an intermediary organization (6). The elements of cooperative intensity were then weighted and adjusted to produce a final score of a fraction of 1. Although all three dimensions of intensity are important in assessing commitment to partnerships through document analysis, they are not all equally weighted. The institutionalization score was weighted the highest, at 45 per cent of the final score, binding was weighted as 35 per cent, and timing 25 per cent. Policy intensity was measured from 0 to 1: mandatory policy areas as 0, necessary policy areas as 0.5, and optional policy areas as 1. In terms of fiscal intensity, values range from 0 to 3. Agreements with no financial commitment were assigned a value of 0, contracted services a value of 1, contracted services with regular payments a value of 2, and agreements that share costs a 3. Risk was also evaluated on a scale or 0 to 3: agreements with third-party or provincial regulation were assigned a value of 0, agreements with penalties for non-compliance a value of 1, agreements with insurance options a value of 2, and agreements with risk mitigation a value of 3. The two elements were then weighted and adjusted to produce a final score of a fraction of 1. Although both dimensions of intensity are important in assessing financial commitment of a partnership, they have not been equally weighted: exchange is weighted at 75 per cent of the final score, while risk is weighted at 25 per cent. Adding policy and fiscal intensity measures provides for a more synthetic approach to the study of inter-local cooperation in Canada and a better understanding of integration mechanisms at the local level. Cooperative, fiscal, and policy intensity measures were calculated for each agreement in the case studies.

The total scores from each CMA in the study are presented in Figure 2.5, separated by category – policy, fiscal, and cooperative intensity. It is clear that none of the CMAs is entering into agreements that substantially integrate operations or bind actors. This means municipalities are not actively attempting to merge service sectors, substantially share resources, or sign agreements in complex policy and service areas. We see interest from municipalities in sharing services, but little desire to integrate government mechanisms, share fiscal resources, or merge policy spaces. Studying agreement intensity also helps to bring context when comparing CMAs. Overall, however, CMAs are signing agreements of relatively low intensity: short term, low cost, and mainly for mandatory policy areas. Despite the transboundary policy environment in which large Canadian metropolitan areas operate, decentralized solutions to servicing dilemmas have not been embraced. Where shared servicing is being explored, municipalities are grasping at low-hanging fruit.

Conclusion

This chapter set out to answer two key research questions: which municipalities are cooperating or contracting? and what service and policy areas are involved? These questions were answered in two ways. The first involved a descriptive approach examining agreements from twelve Canadian CMAs. The second used an intensity scale to explore the degree of binding involved with the collected agreements. Some interesting findings emerge.

Figure 2.5. Average Agreement Intensity by Census Metropolitan Area

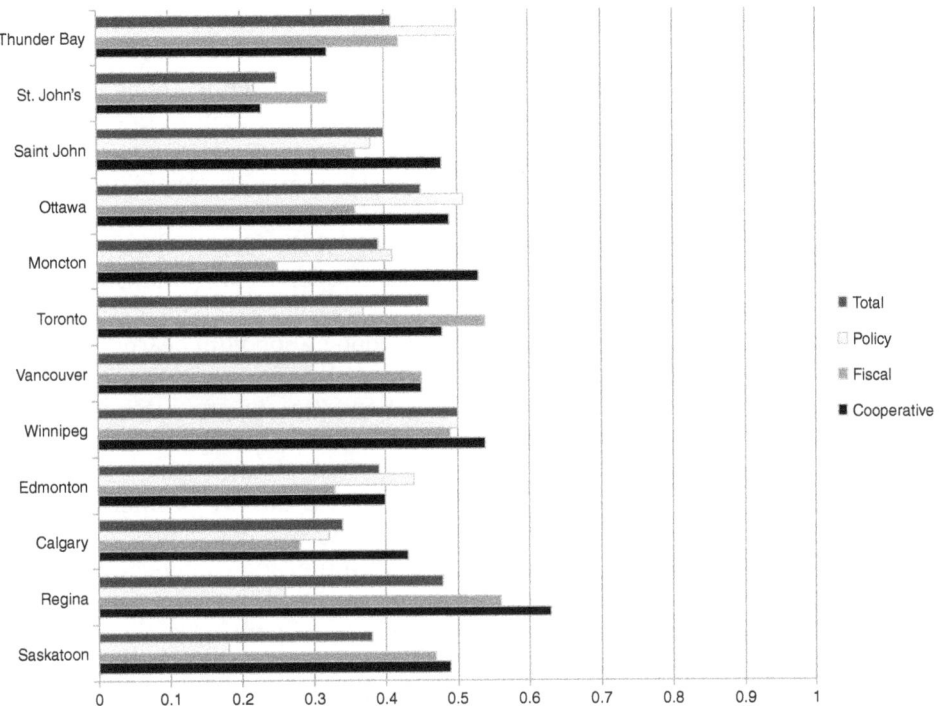

Source: Author's compilation.

The first involves the rate of agreement formation. Canadian municipalities share or contract services with others less than elsewhere in the world. The number of agreements uncovered in the selected sample, 648, is a surprising finding given the size and complexity of the CMAs involved. In comparison, US studies examining interlocal agreement formation typically uncover hundreds, if not thousands, of agreements within metropolitan areas. For instance, Shrestha (2005) found 6,080 agreements among 38 large US cities; Wood (2005) found 1,638 different agreements in the Kansas City metropolitan area; Thurmaier (2005) similarly located nearly 12,000 agreements signed between 1965 and 2004 in Iowa; LeRoux and Carr (2007) discovered 445 road agreements in Michigan; and Andrew (2008) found 390 public safety agreements in Florida. The number of agreements in Canadian metropolitan areas pales in comparison.

A natural question to pose in light of these results is, why? The most apparent explanation is a provincial emphasis on creating larger municipalities and the search for institutional solutions to local servicing dilemmas. Hence, provincial governments have looked to amalgamation and annexation before seriously examining the merits of intermunicipal cooperation. As such, we have seen massive amalgamations and annexations in some of Canada's largest city-regions, including Toronto (Frisken 2007), Winnipeg (Higgins 1986; Sancton 2000), Calgary (Foran 2009), and Edmonton (Lesage Jr. 2005). As borders are extended outwards, there is less need for interlocal cooperation. In the United States, metropolitan areas are much more fragmented, which means there are not only more opportunities for cooperation with nearby municipalities, but also much more need.

Aside from pushing institutional solutions, certain provinces have even actively dissuaded local governments from forming intermunicipal partnerships. As just one example, a 1987 Ontario government report, entitled *Patterns for the Future,* described the use of interlocal agreements as problematic. Noting that interlocal agreements can be "time-consuming to negotiate, can foster dispute, and can create confusion about accountability," the report argued that these agreements create uncertainty about lines of policy-making responsibility (Ontario 1987, 62).[14] Interlocal agreements, the report continues, do not necessarily provide stable administration since their terms and conditions are subject to periodic re-negotiation (65). I explore the explanations for lower levels of interlocal cooperation and contracting in greater detail in the final chapter.

Most of the agreements collected for the sample are for emergency services – areas of necessity for municipalities. Many of these are mutual-aid agreements, meaning they are in force only in case of emergency. These are low-risk agreements intended to grant permission for other municipal emergency services to assist a community that is not their own. Of the sample as a whole, most agreements are contracts and most are restrictive, and thus come with legal protection, which might indicate a low level of trust between some municipal governments. Although it is difficult to grasp fully just how many informal agreements exist within the CMAs selected for the sample, past research (see Spicer 2016b) indicates that this practice is sparse and largely on the wane. Most municipalities opt for the legal protections that formal agreements provide.

As for intensity, few higher-order agreements make concerted efforts to integrate administration and service delivery. For the most part, municipalities in the sample are not entering into agreements that substantially integrate operations or bind actors to one another. Most agreements have easy termination clauses, which limit long-term integration. Municipalities are not actively attempting to merge service sectors, substantially share resources, or sign agreements in complex policy or service areas.

The following chapter builds upon these findings and explains how the cooperative process unfolds, including the factors that lead municipalities to cooperate or contract with one another.

3 Explaining Cooperation

In the previous chapter, I explored the local cooperative landscape in Canada by examining the interlocal agreements collected from twelve Census Metropolitan Areas. The results showed that, while municipalities within these Canadian CMAs are cooperating and contracting with their peers less than in other countries, such as the United States, they are undoubtedly sharing or contracting a range of services, some of them critical services, such as water and transit. By examining the intensity of these arrangements, it was shown that Canadian municipalities also are not seeking to integrate administrative structures. Instead, municipalities in the CMAs examined in the previous chapter are signing short-term, purpose-driven agreements.

While the previous chapter provided a high-level overview of the cooperative landscape, this chapter delves deeper into the reasons municipalities cooperate, exploring the incentives and motivations for cooperation, the underlying rationales for pursuing arrangements, and the timing of cooperative actions.

The Calculus of Cooperation

The question of why municipalities choose to cooperate or contract with others is an intriguing one. For the most part, municipalities have the tools they need to deliver services to their residents independently of one another. Indeed, there are many reasons not to cooperate or contract with another municipality. One partner might fail to meet expectations and the agreement could end up in court. Relationships with other municipalities could sour if things go poorly. Cooperation and service sharing could actually cost a municipality more if not done properly. Monitoring or enforcing the agreement might take up too much staff time. The agreement might not have the support of the public. Perhaps the service provided is of poor quality or below previous standards. The list could go on – there is no shortage of reasons to doubt that a particular agreement might be effective. Risk is involved in every potential cooperative or contractual relationship among municipalities.

The previous chapter showed that municipalities are willing to accept a degree of risk and move forwards with some type of cooperative relationship – albeit with less frequency than one might expect. What gets municipal decision makers to the point where they believe the benefits of cooperation outweigh the risks? A number of considerations have to be taken in account, but the initial decision rests on two main conditions that need to be satisfied in order to start the cooperative process: willingness and capacity.[1] Willingness refers to the desire to cooperate and could relate back to a need to create a new service or improve an existing one. Capacity refers to the ability to cooperate. Unless both conditions are satisfied, interlocal cooperation has no starting point.

As Table 3.1 shows, the first condition is closely tied to the motivations mentioned above: municipalities must be willing to cooperate. There needs to be a clear benefit, and the motivations in this category are not based purely on strict rational-choice assumptions. Certainly, transaction costs need to be low and the possibility of efficiency gains or cost savings need to be present, but a number of political and interpersonal conditions must also be satisfied, such as council support and a history of cooperation and communication.

Second, cooperation hinges upon capacity. Willingness is certainly a motivator to pursue cooperation, but capacity also determines the process of cooperation. For cooperation or contracting to occur, municipalities must be able to enter into an arrangement. A municipality cannot pursue an agreement adequately if it does not have sufficient resources to negotiate, fund, or monitor the agreement. Municipal governments cannot partner on capital investments without adequate financial or administrative resources. Political constraints are as important as institutional constraints, since political actors must come to agreement easily and be unencumbered by council indecision.

If these initial conditions are met, existing literature on interlocal cooperation tells us a number of generalized and specific motivations and incentives play roles in the decision-making process. Filipe Teles, in his 2016 book, *Local Governance and Inter-Municipal Cooperation*, argues that these motivations and incentives may occur at a number of scales and include assumptions that are made *a priori* and *a posteriori*. In such cases, certain events in the past and the nature of the problem itself – *a priori* – might affect the incentive to cooperate. The history of interaction and cooperation in the past might impact the way certain

The second incentive for interlocal cooperation is to help municipalities fill service gaps (Warner 2015). Some municipalities are unable to deliver certain services to residents. An example is water: some municipalities might not have access to enough source water for the entire community.[4] Partnering with another municipality to provide the service would help ensure service continuity and overcome problems of geographic and environmental isolation that might limit community size. Closely related to this are capacity and scale. If a municipality does not have the capacity to deliver a service on its own, doing so jointly or under contract with another municipality might be the right solution. For instance, if a small, growing municipality is located next to a major city, it might be able to contract an extension of transit lines from the major municipality instead of starting its own transit service, which would have high initial costs.[5] For the larger municipality, extending bus service would have a much lower cost given that the infrastructure is already in place.

In fact, such a transit extension might increase service quality for residents of both communities, which leads to the third incentive: municipalities might be able to increase the quality of services they provide by cooperating with others (Post 2004; Warner 2015). Cooperation with another municipality not only allows a government to invest more in service production or delivery; it also allows local actors to tap into the perhaps greater policy expertise and skills of those employed by partner municipalities.

The fourth major incentive is to control externalities. Municipalities in close proximity to one another often experience common servicing or policy dilemmas. Growth and development, for example, often spill over borders, creating a need for common policy cooperation or regional growth initiatives. Transportation continuity is another externality that often needs to be managed. People can move from one municipality to another for work, leaving an impact on infrastructure. Creating mechanisms to manage these externalities jointly can avoid the long-term fiscal burden of improper planning. Cooperation might help monitor shared natural resources, such as transboundary waterways, or at the very least, improve the incentives of those with a stake in shared resources to devote more attention to their health and protection.

Finally, municipalities can be forced or coerced into cooperating with other municipalities by government mandate, although these service mandates are rare. One example is Ontario's Consolidated Municipal Service Manger (CMSM) system, introduced in 1998 as part of the Local Service Realignment Act (Ontario 1998), which provided increased responsibility for social assistance, childcare, social housing, land ambulance services, and public health to municipalities. The overall goal was to create an integrated service delivery framework for core social service programming, while "rationalizing" the fiscal responsibility for servicing between the provincial government and municipalities (Spicer 2015a). To ensure these services were delivered effectively and equitably, the province established 37 consolidated municipal service managers and 10 northern district social services administrative boards, each of which roughly aligned with previously existing jurisdictions.

The province automatically assigned responsibility for CMSM services to most municipalities. Upper-tier governments – such as regional, county, and district governments – were mandated to be the service managers. Single-tier municipalities outside of two-tier systems would be responsible for CMSM servicing unless otherwise assigned to another catchment area by the province. This arrangement covered the majority of municipalities in the province. Counties with separated cities, however, were not given a mandate determining which level of government would be responsible for CMSM servicing. The province provided them with a broad range of decision-making authority to determine whether the county or the city – areas without institutional linkages – would be responsible for the delivery and administration of CMSM services and create a local funding arrangement. The inclusion of this provision made certain areas across the province with a separated city-county structure come to their own agreement on the funding and delivery of CMSM services. As a result, several areas wound up in arbitration, which in some cases damaged relationships for many years.[6]

Mandated cooperation has a range of challenges, but is seen infrequently in Canada. For the most part, interlocal cooperation and contracting in Canada is voluntary, with a range of factors prompting municipalities at least to consider cooperating or contracting with one another. Many of these revolve around a desire to improve the efficiency and quality of local services, but political factors also come into play when local councils decide on whether to pursue cooperative arrangements.

Examining the Calculus of Cooperation

Existing literature examining the incentives to pursue interlocal cooperation and contracting is quite rich. From this work, we know a great deal about the calculations that municipal practitioners and politicians confront during the cooperative or contracting decision-making process. This section of the chapter examines some of the responses of practitioners from the August 2015 survey of municipal officials in Ontario. As mentioned in the introductory chapter, this particular survey delved much deeper into the attitudes and motivations of practitioners to sign interlocal agreements than the one administered by the Ontario Ministry of Municipal Affairs and Housing in 2012. The 2015 survey received 707 responses from senior staff and politicians in small, medium, and large municipalities across the province. Respondents were asked to gauge their experience with past cooperative activity (if they engaged in any) and rate their proclivity towards future cooperation under certain scenarios.

Figure 3.1 displays the reasons respondents cited to pursue cooperative arrangements with other municipalities.

The most popular rationales are the potential to lower costs, increase service efficiency, and improve service coordination. This is in line with existing literature, but past research is mixed on how much interlocal cooperation actually might achieve these goals. Despite a lack of consensus, municipal governments continue to pursue cooperative and contractual relationships on this basis, hoping to find efficiency gains and cost reductions along the way. Among survey respondents, 74 per cent either agreed or strongly agreed that interlocal cooperation saves governments money. In contrast, only 5.5 per cent of respondents disagreed with the statement, while 20 per cent neither agreed or disagreed. In terms of service quality, 71 per cent of those surveyed either agreed or strongly agreed with the statement that interlocal cooperation improved service quality, 24 per cent neither agreed nor disagreed, while only 3 per cent disagreed or strongly disagreed; less than 2 per cent indicated they were unsure.

Surprisingly, an inability to deliver a service alone is much farther down the list in terms of priorities for municipal officials. A little over 20 per cent of respondents indicated this was a main rationale for them to pursue cooperation or contracting with another government. Respondents who did list this as a priority were mainly from small or rural municipalities, which could indicate that they operate in governments with a much more constrained capacity and scope. Within these environments, innovations in service delivery might be much more naturally appealing for productivity-maximizing administrators or budget-conscious politicians.

The demands of residents are at the bottom of the scale: about 10 per cent of respondents indicated resident demand was a motivator for pursuing interlocal cooperation. This might appear surprising, but residents' demands for service in general are usually top-of-mind for politicians and officials. If a particular municipality did not have a fire service or a road maintenance department, residents understandably would be concerned about safety and the conditions of their roads. The demand, however, would be to provide the service in general, not the

Figure 3.1. Reasons to Cooperate

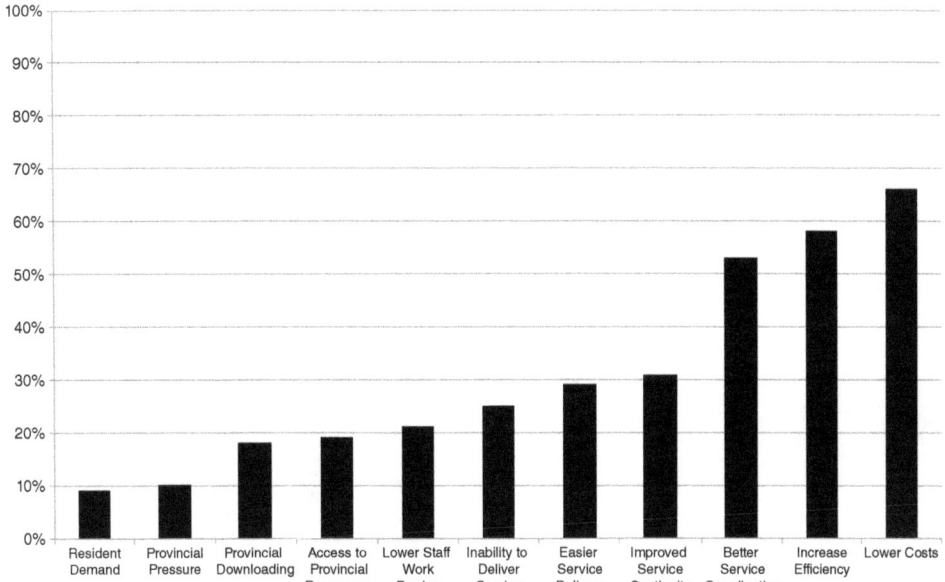

method of provision. It is hard to imagine residents of a community demanding their local councillors pursue a cooperative agreement on fire servicing or road maintenance. The details of service provisions usually are not a large concern for residents, as long as they are provided, which one can presume is why "resident demand" is such a low priority.

The demands of residents also might manifest themselves within the preference order of administrators and politicians in other ways. As shown above, respondents indicated that lowering costs and increasing service efficiency were the main drivers for pursuing cooperative or contractual activity with another municipality, and politicians might be acting on residents' demands about the fiscal health of their municipality in these areas. Whether a service is contracted or delivered jointly is likely not as important as whether it is delivered adequately.

Turning from general motivations, municipal decision makers also must be concerned about potential partners. Much like anyone entering a business venture, the characteristics and history of potential partners matter, and provide an indication about how they might conduct themselves within a partnership or business venture. Municipal governments approach potential relationships in the same manner. Figure 3.2

Figure 3.2. Qualities in Partnership

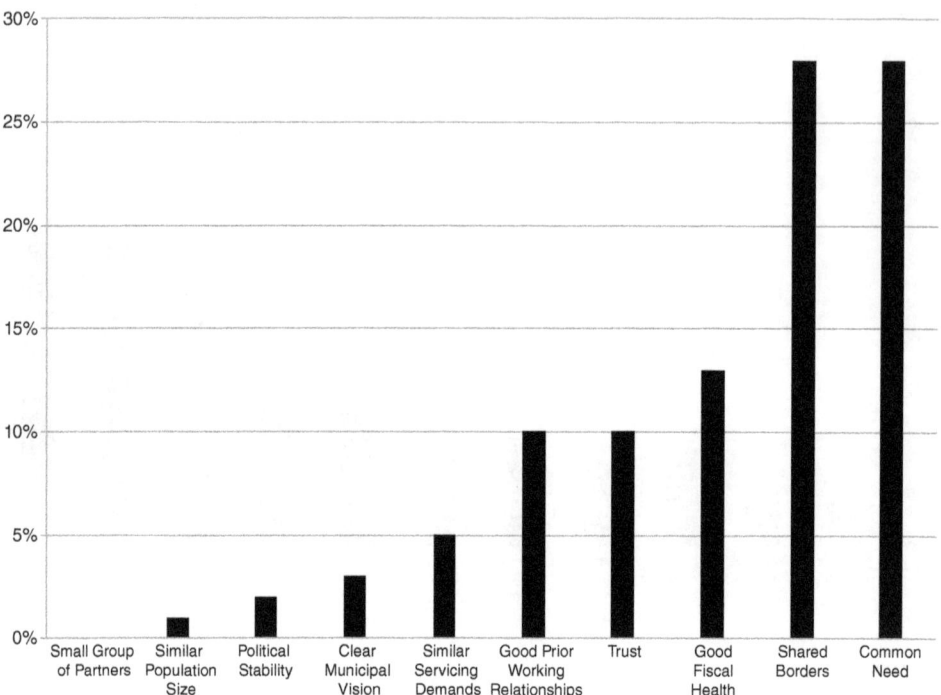

and 3.3 display the types of qualities respondents sought and avoided when considering forming cooperative arrangements.

Figure 3.2 shows the types of qualities respondents considered important when considering intermunicipal cooperation and contracting arrangements. The two most important categories were a common need – meaning two municipalities share a need to deliver a service or have a common servicing problem they could both help to solve – and a shared border. A common need generally establishes a basis for cooperation; it can be seen as the building block of cooperative and contractual relationships. Need also tends to set the tone for the relationship between the parties involved in the arrangements. With both (or more) parties aware they are experiencing common challenges, they enter relationships on roughly equal footing. A common need removes any potential power imbalance.

Given the importance of proximity in shared and contractual servicing, it should not be too surprising that respondents considered a

Figure 3.3. Characteristics Dissuading Cooperation

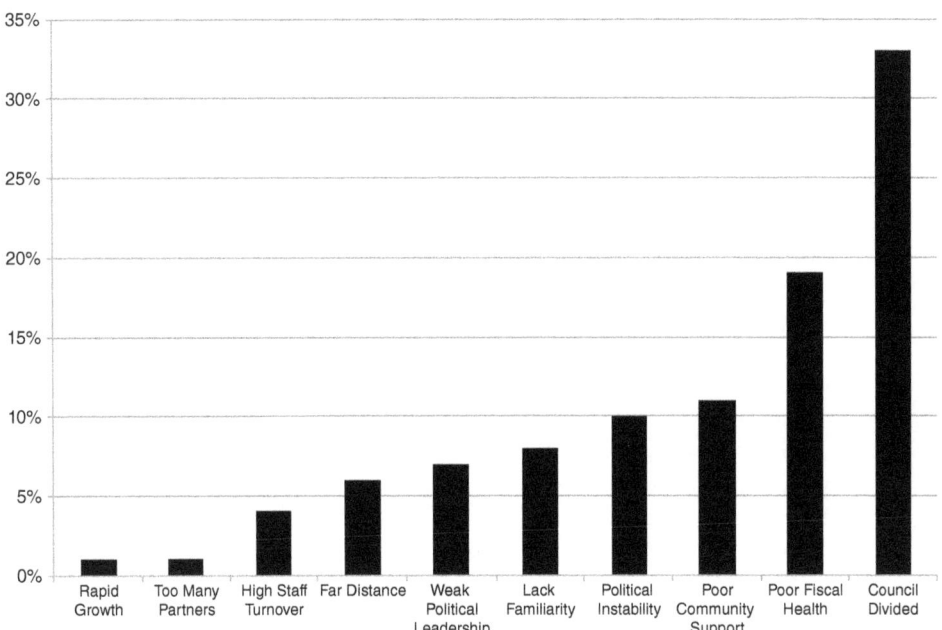

shared border so important. In fact, borders can create opportunity and challenge for municipalities. For instance, a shared border might put municipal actors into more frequent conversation, which can increase the chances of cooperation. Communication breeds trust, and a shared border can be the catalyst for this process. Municipalities, of course, cannot pick their neighbours, so a shared border increases the chances local actors will accommodate one another or, at the very least, work to maintain a healthy relationship. By contrast, a shared border can also create challenges, in that negative externalities might force municipalities to work together to mitigate potential hardship. It can also set off challenges related to growth and development, as municipalities on one side of the border might be more sensitive to growth taking place in other communities (see Spicer 2016a). Additionally, cooperating with municipalities a distance away creates a host of coordination challenges for local administrators. In any case, whether a shared border produces challenges or opportunities, the literature on interlocal cooperation tells us that it increases the likelihood of cooperation. The survey results confirm those findings.

Respondents also identified good fiscal health and trust as important factors in establishing cooperative and contractual relationships with other municipalities. Both have also been identified as key factors in past research. Municipal administrators look for stability when seeking partnerships, and good fiscal health is a solid indicator of stability. Municipal actors might view another municipality with good fiscal health as a potential partner concerned with fiscal prudence and adhering to widely accepted best practices in administration. In contrast, a municipality running continuous deficits or pursuing too many projects might be seen as unstable or undisciplined and unnecessarily risky. Good fiscal health is also a sign that a potential partner has the resources to cooperate – meaning it is unlikely that one municipality will end up absorbing more of the cost of cooperation.

Trust is also an important factor, as it demonstrates to municipalities that they can work together if there is long-standing familiarity. At the most basic level, we want to work with those we trust. We intrinsically feel more comfortable in these types of partnerships. Where trust is high, risk is generally low. The same can be said for municipalities. On a more practical level, trust also reduces the need for monitoring an arrangement. If we trust those we work with, there is less reason to worry about the actions of partners. This ultimately lowers the cost of the agreement, leading to potential efficiency gains.

Figure 3.3 presents a range of factors that could dissuade municipal actors from pursuing cooperative arrangements, according to survey respondents. The most frequent response was a divided council. Other municipalities might interpret this as a sign of instability, which could mean that the municipality might terminate an agreement early, thereby injecting additional risk into a potential intermunicipal agreement. Again, this is in line with the top responses for cooperative action. Municipalities seek stability in partners, and a divided council gives some reason for pause and creates doubt that a municipality might change its policy priorities. The second most cited factor was poor fiscal health. Again, municipalities might interpret this a risk factor, potentially leading to a municipality's terminating an agreement or failing to fulfil its financial obligations because of a lack of funds.

The survey data also provided the impressions of respondents whose municipality had cooperative agreements in place. The vast majority of these were formal agreements. In fact, almost 70 per cent of respondents indicated they had only formal agreements, while less than 2 per cent had only informal agreements; 29 per cent indicated they had both in place, but the mix of agreements was unclear. Of those with formal agreements in place, 34 per cent had between 1 and 3 agreements, 47 percent had 4 to 7 in place, 11 per cent had 8 to 10 in place, 3 per cent had 11 to 15 in place, and 5 per cent had 16 or more agreements in place.

Respondents were asked to rate the interlocal agreements they had in place using a 7-point Likert scale across four dimensions: overall experience, satisfaction, communication with other agreement partners, and agreement effectiveness. The average for each dimension was over 5, indicating that respondents were generally quite satisfied with their agreements.

Although satisfaction was high, that does not mean challenges do not occur, and in the next chapter, I explore agreement failure and ask why and how interlocal agreements and interlocal relationships unravel and get terminated. Respondents with agreements in place or who had used them in the past, however, reported few challenges. In fact, no individual challenge was reported by more than 30 per cent of respondents. The four highest responses – partner commitment level, staff changes, financial disagreements, and communication – warrant a closer look.

When an agreement is signed, most aspects are covered, including financial exchange and resource allocation. Over time, however, enthusiasm for the agreement might change in one municipality. Although the terms of the contract might not technically be broken, the desire to improve the working relationship might suffer if both parties are not fully committed to its success. This partial breakdown can have a range of effects, from not returning phone calls or addressing problems collectively to delays in delivering payments and requests to renegotiate the agreement. Again, these impacts might not be fatal, but they are certainly frustrating.

Also frustrating, but a fact of life as in every organization, are staff changes. Most agreements have a designated staff member who provides a contact point for a counterpart in another community. If that person leaves or if organizational responsibility shifts, it might take time to train someone new or a particular replacement might not share the same interest or enthusiasm in the agreement.

The third most frequently cited challenge was financial disagreement. As mentioned above, financial commitments are often spelled out in the agreements themselves, but over time the nature or scale of the service might change. In some cases – such as waste management or water delivery – the scale of the service is always dynamic, as usage rates are difficult to predetermine. When these financial commitments need adjustment, one party might disagree. Occasionally, arbitration is necessary. Again, these types of disagreements are not necessarily fatal.

Finally, respondents also reported communication challenges. Sometimes this can come in the form of miscommunication or a failure to communicate at all. Communication, as noted previously, builds trust and aids in the process of reaching cooperative agreements. If this communication is not carried through the execution of an agreement, it could pose challenges and create frustration on both sides.

Overall, municipalities are searching for stable partners that share a common need or desire to work together. With all partnerships, actors work to minimize risk. Municipalities are similar in this regard: poor fiscal health and divisions on council are just some of the reasons municipal officials avoid working with others. When agreements are signed, however, they are generally viewed favourably: few survey respondents indicated serious challenges.

What about the Private Sector?

One aspect that routinely emerges during discussions about interlocal cooperation in Canada is the private sector. If municipalities are contracting with each other, why not simply contract with the private sector instead? Why would a local government prefer to work with another local government instead of a private firm?

The most common form of service delivery for municipalities is referred to as direct production, whereby the unit of government that makes basic tax and expenditure decisions produces a particular service (Ostrom, Bish, and Ostrom 1988). With direct production, a municipality relies upon its own staff and supplies to produce a service, and charges residents accordingly. Municipalities, of course, do not need to deliver every service they produce (Oakerson 1999). Contracting to the private sector has shown to produce benefits, mostly through cost efficiencies, for local governments, which gives the concept some intuitive appeal (Bel and Warner 2008; Dachis 2010; Hefetz and Warner 2007; McDavid 2000). Certain authors and local practitioners, however, have raised concerns about contracting with the private sector, such as unstable long-term dynamics, a lack of service provision accountability, and the carrying of too much risk by the public sector (Ohemeng and Grant 2008; van Slyke 2003).

The advantages sought in the full or partial privatization of public services stem from competition in provision (Warner 2012). Simply put, private firms compete for business, meaning local governments can benefit from the competitive dynamics among firms. It is also widely believed that the private sector has lower production costs than the public sector, which inevitably would produce cost savings for municipal governments (Bel and Fageda 2006; Wassenaar, Dijkgraaf, and Gradus 2010). One particular private contractor might provide the same service in different municipalities, thereby allowing fixed costs to be shared among municipalities, which generates economies of scale (Donahue 1989). The evidence of cost savings, however, is somewhat mixed (Bel and Warner 2008; Boyne 1998; Hodge 2000). Some studies have found cost reductions through private contracting (Benito, Solana, and Morena 2014; Reeves and Barrow 2000; Simões, Cruz, and Marques 2012). Others have found higher costs (Ohlsson 2003; Stevens 1978; Zafra-Gómez et al. 2013). The differences in these results can be attributed to a number of factors, including a lack of competition, early exhaustion of any economies of scale, and inadequate accounting of costs (Bel and Warner 2015). Scale also might play a role. Some studies have found that rural municipalities use contracting less, mainly because fewer private providers are available in rural areas, which decreases the benefits derived from competition (Bel and Fageda 2011; Johnston and Girth 2012; Warner 2006; Warner and Hefetz 2002).

Few studies have directly compared contracting with the private sector to contracting or cooperating among municipalities. In his 2010 study on waste contracting, Dachis found mixed results – namely, that it did not matter if waste disposal and diversion services were contracted out to another municipality or to a private firm in terms of cost savings, but there were noticeable differences when it came to collection services. When municipalities contracted with a private company for collection, they realized cost savings of 24 per cent, a marked improvement over arrangements with other municipal governments (Dachis 2010, 13). Such evidence certainly suggests that savings in interlocal contracting depend on the nature of the service offered. Dachis provides some possible explanations for these findings: the higher productivity of private workers, wage and benefit savings, and the better use of technology by private contractors. Providing concrete linkages between these findings, however, was beyond the scope of his project.

Why do some municipalities opt for intermunicipal contracting and service sharing rather than private contracting? First, public organizations do not have the same incentive to eke out profit (Dollery and Johnson 2005; Feiock 2007; Henderson 2015). As such, some municipal actors believe that public servicing leads to increased attention to the quality of services and delivery and more recourse to rectifying problems in the event of a dispute over the arrangement. Second, there is a great deal of flexibility in interlocal arrangements, where a variety of potential relationships exists. For example, co-management of a service is a potentially attractive concept to local partners that is not possible with private contracting. Service swapping, where one municipality trades responsibility for one service for another service with a neighbouring government, might have the same effect. The range of governance options could be intriguing to local actors, but the explanation might simply boil down to politics – with local officials wary of contracting with the private sector because of optics. Municipal governments, therefore, might prefer contracting with other governments, as opposed to private vendors, because governments share common interests in service delivery, ultimately making government a more trusted service vendor (Brown 2008; Marvel and Marvel 2008). Intermunicipal relationships might be seen as less controversial with voters and, therefore, more palatable to local political actors.

Cooperation and Competition as Strategy

Does cooperation come naturally for municipalities? Within the private sector, competition is the norm, from which consumers expect to benefit. For the most part, we do not have the same expectations of public bodies. The notion of two hospitals or schools undercutting each other for patients or students is hard to imagine when both are publicly funded. Public institutions, however, have been shown to compete – albeit on a much more limited scale than the private sector (Brennan and Buchanan 1980; Chai and Treisman 2004; Qian and Roland 1998) – which has drawn the criticism of those who argue that competition prompts local governments to exploit spillovers and export taxes or pollution to neighbouring jurisdictions (Gordon 1983; Oates and Schwab 1988). Others argue that competition among local governments can create a "race-to-the-bottom" mindset in terms of tax rates and regulation (Keen and Marchand 1997). Many have also argued, however, that competition between governments at all levels can be beneficial and ought to be encouraged (Mankiw 2012; Oates 1972; Schnurer 2013). Even with these competitive dynamics in play – and regardless of whether one argues competition is inherently positive or negative – it is possible to cooperate.

A key division in the academic literature about metropolitan governance involves those described as either consolidationists or public choice theorists. Simply put, consolidationists view metropolitan areas as fundamentally chaotic and unworkable and, as a result, advocate for institutions that reach the edge of the region. Tools such as annexation and amalgamation help to achieve this goal and to ensure that metropolitan areas reside within one government institution. Public choice scholars, on the other hand, view the fragmentation of metropolitan areas as functional, and argue that a host of local governments within one metropolitan area provides more choice and value for residents.

Central to this debate is competition. Both groups of theorists acknowledge there is a great deal of competition within metropolitan areas, but disagree fundamentally about the value of such competition. Consolidationists argue that this competition is counterproductive, leading to inevitable tension and ultimately hurting the region. Those adhering to the consolidationist perspective view those living within a metropolitan area as sharing a set of common interests that bind them together as one community. Only a single, unified government, they argue, could properly aggregate these interests without devolving into conflict (Gulick 1962; Warren 1966). Although early consolidationist arguments centred around finding efficiency in service delivery and streamlining administrative organization (Anderson 1925; Jones 1942; Studenski 1930),[7] creating and maintaining organizations that could properly insulate and manage conflict became the prime focus for many later consolidationist thinkers (see, for example, Banfield 1957; Bollens 1973; Hobbs 1971; Magulof 1975; Zimmerman 1970).[8]

In contrast to the consolidationists, public choice theorists, view competition among local governments as functional. Public choice theory holds the individual at its foundation. Individuals are presumed to have a preference for certain goods and services and a knowledge – which is assumed to be imperfect – of alternatives that might be available to them (Bish and Ostrom 1973; Buchanan and Tullock 1962; Ostrom and Ostrom 1971; Tullock 1965). Within a local government, citizens have a number of venues to express these preferences, and try to get local decisions to align with their desires (Sproule-Jones 1974; Sproule-Jones and Hart 1973). Perhaps the best option, however, is to "vote with their feet," and seek out a community that best represents their preferences for how local services ought to be delivered and the tax rates they are willing to pay for such services (Tiebout 1956). Bish and Ostrom (1973, 30) provide us with an overview of this process:

> If a citizen is dissatisfied with the benefits received from the local government where he resides he can simply move to a governmental unit where the level and mix of services relative to the tax payments comes closer to meeting his preferences. Most metropolitan areas contain many different local government jurisdictions. Suburbanization in metropolitan areas may well reflect citizen dissatisfaction with the high costs and poor services rendered in central cities. If a person feels that good schools are important for his children and he cannot afford the tuition of private schools, the solution may be to move to a suburban school district where his family can secure the education he wants.

From the public choice school of thought, we have the basic calculus of citizen movement. If the municipality in which one is currently residing is providing poor quality services or is levying too high a tax for those services (according to the determination made by the individual, of course), the resident will seek out another jurisdiction where those services can be obtained at a higher quality or at a lower tax rate. Consolidation of these local units reduces competition and, thus, consumer choice.

It should be noted, however, that arguments supporting a "vote-with-your-feet" mentality in local politics have been somewhat tempered over the years. Critics note that movement is not easy (Lucy 1975; Varady and Raffel 1995). Selling your property and moving to another municipality because your current municipality does not perfectly match your preference order is not always possible or logical. No one makes this argument more forcefully than William Fischel in *The Homevoter Hypothesis* (2001), where he makes a convincing case that residents will choose "voice" (voting, communicating with decision makers, and other forms of local participation) over "exit." Whereas Tiebout (1956) argued that "exit" is a homeowner's primary option in the face of undesirable politics, Fischel (2001, 12) points out that such a strategy is far from effortless, and can have negative economic repercussions for homeowners, such as selling one's home at a loss if market conditions are not optimal. Additionally, homeowners might have bonds with a certain community or close family within a certain area that they are unwilling to leave. Leaving a municipality because of high taxes or low-quality services is one option available to residents, but not one entered into lightly – as Fischel (2001) suggests, some might simply stay and try to change their local government by using their "voice."

Local actors operate with the knowledge that residents might leave their communities and seek out municipalities that better suit their needs and preferences. Municipal leaders thus often seek out competitive advantage in the hope of retaining and enhancing local populations, which ultimately make their communities more attractive destinations. Improving the quality of local services or providing them at a lower cost, through either public or private contracting, can be one method of achieving a local competitive advantage (Bish and Ostrom 1973).

The preceding chapters discussed how Canadian metropolitan areas are much less fragmented than their US counterparts. A primary reason for this trend is that provincial governments have a consolidationist streak, and have aggressively pursued amalgamation and annexations – strategies that undoubtedly are favoured by consolidationist thinkers. How does this affect local competition? Canadian metropolitan areas still feature competition, largely because municipal governments are prone to certain competitive instincts. Local actors in Canadian cities, much like those in US cities, still covet certain local goods, such as increased population, tourists, new business, and government resources. Regardless of the size of the market, competition still exists, although it takes a different shape and form within Canadian CMAs.

Lucy and Phillips argue that competition between municipalities is extensive, but mostly focuses on the outward appearance of a community and the strength of municipal scope and capacity: "competition includes struggle by local government officials to retain and attract residents of sufficient means to pay taxes, invest in housing, purchase goods and services, populate public schools and enforce norms of public conduct" (2000, 15). Municipalities compete for certain types of residents, businesses, and non-profit organizations that are more attractive and prized than others because they possess certain strategic resources, such as jobs, property value, income, education, skills, civic virtue, or family support (Asheim and Isaksen 1997; Begg 2002; Deas and Giordano 2002; Kresl 2002; Wolfe and Bramwell 2008). This competitive desire operates at a number of scales, as cities seek a competitive advantage not only locally, but also globally (Florida 2012; Graham 2002; Hollands 2008). Cities also seek to diversify their populations – for example, by attracting middle-class families that might have moved to the suburbs in previous years (Varady and Raffel 1995).

Schneider (1989) provides a simplified model of local "buyers" and "sellers." To Schneider, metropolitan areas are just like any type of marketplace, where certain actors bring goods to market in the hope others will purchase them at a certain price. In Schneider's conceptual marketplace, the "buyers" are people and businesses that choose to reside in the communities of any particular metropolitan area. These buyers choose to locate in one municipality over the other and, as a result, pay for their choice through taxes to their local government. These buyers have certain "tastes," which influence their decision to locate (or not to locate) in a particular municipality. These "tastes" could include a preference for a variety of local goods and amenities, such as green space, transit, libraries, and increased police protection. Buyers, Schneider (1989) argues, want to purchase these products at the lowest price possible.

The "sellers" in Schneider's marketplace are local governments. He explains: "within each local government, politicians and bureaucrats are the decision-makers with primary responsibility for assembling the particular package of goods and services offered by each municipality ... municipalities present a 'bundle' (or product mix) of goods and services to buyers, among which firms and residents choose" (Schneider

1989, 8). The types of goods up for "sale" are diverse, but ultimately, if municipalities can get people and businesses to buy, they can enhance their position and grow. Much of this is in line with the incentives for private firms: more "sales" will grow the firm. When municipalities become more focused on achieving these types of gains, they often adopt a competitive lens, seeing others, especially those with similar goals, as direct competition (Begg 1999; Parkinson and Boddy 2004; Young 2012). Regional cooperation on highly coveted items, such as local investment, is unlikely (Young 2012).[9]

The mentality around this competition is self-reinforcing. Growth is seen as intrinsically good, is rarely questioned, and is often supported through a local "booster spirit" (Boorstin 1965). Municipalities often actively market themselves to send both internal and external signals of strength and prosperity, with the end goal of increasing their competitive position relative to regional and national peers (Asworth and Voogd 1990; Duffy 1995; Gold and Ward 1994; Harvey and Young 2012; Smyth 1994).[10] In their seminal 1987 work, *Urban Fortunes*, Logan and Molotch elaborate on this celebration of local growth: "schoolchildren are taught to view local history as a series of breakthroughs in the expansion of the economic base of their city and region, celebrating its numerical leadership in one sort of production or another; more generally, increases in population tend to be equated with local progress" (61).[11] Caught up in this enthusiasm, municipal politicians and administrators exercise policies to help their municipality expand and grow. With this growth mentality, it becomes natural to see other governments as potential rivals.

Within this mixed metropolitan marketplace are public actors (politicians and administrators) and private actors – "place entrepreneurs" as Logan and Molotch (1987) might term them – who set and reinforce a competitive mentality. The goods they compete for can be placed in three categories: population, business and industry, and external resources.

Competition for population: As the old adage goes, there is strength in numbers. From a local government standpoint, higher populations are often seen as a competitive advantage (Begg 2002). A city with a high population is perceived to be more attractive to those from outside the area; a municipality with a larger population is perceived to come with a ready supply of attractive local goods (Lucy and Phillips 2000; Varady and Raffel 1995). Firms prefer to settle in areas where there is not only a potential workforce, but also a potential market for their products (Boddy and Parkinson 2004). A large population is also attractive to individual residents, as it provides an opportunity to create larger social networks and interact with others. A large population also might translate into greater potential for employers, making it attractive for outsiders seeking work and other opportunities (Moore and Begg 2004). Population increase, therefore, is seen as a sign of increasing strength: more people are settling in the city, projecting an image of inherent attractiveness to outsiders. With this mindset in place, municipal politicians and administrators will often devote a great deal of resources and energy to attracting new residents.[12]

Competition for business and industry: Aside from people, municipal administrators and politicians also covet business and industry. Capital is increasingly mobile, providing cities with more incentive to retain and attract new industry (Graham 2002; Hollands 2008; Turok 2005). New business is perceived to bring new jobs, which in turn attracts more residents and other associated services, such as increased activity in the services sector. Business attraction also might be prestigious. An increase in business and industry locating in one community can help cities stave off economic stagnation and sustain themselves during times of economic downturn (Duffy 1995). Commercial and industrial activity is often perceived as an insurance policy against economic decline. Many communities take pride in being home to a certain sectoral cluster, such as Waterloo Region's technology cluster. Many cities build a brand around these sectors (Bramwell, Nelles, and Wolfe 2008). Ultimately, more business activity creates more economic activity and a boost to the local assessment base.

Competition for external resources: Municipalities also compete for a variety of external resources. These include the placement of federal government offices, colleges, universities, prisons, and military bases (Logan and Molotch 1987). This competition also might centre on infrastructure items such as the placement of highways or railway tracks, which give a municipality better access to raw materials, a gateway to sell goods to other markets, and transportation links for residents (Glaab 1962; Scheiber 1973). The federal and provincial governments also distribute grants and allotments of funding to municipalities, which can be used to subsidize the cost of local services or to enhance services (Schneider 1989). Local governments not only need the capacity to accept such grants; they also need to convince other levels of government they would use them effectively. Essentially, cities must make a case for themselves, meaning that they are in competition with other municipalities for scarce provincial and federal resources. As Schneider argues, by forcing municipalities to compete for public funds, upper levels of government essentially "affect the market behavior of local governments" (1989, 7).

The goods contained in each of these categories build the local assessment base, ultimately enhancing the municipal government's fiscal position. A larger population base, coupled with robust commercial and industrial sectors, can increase property taxes and ultimately local "wealth" (Schneider 1989). Those resources can be invested in the community, creating more opportunity that outsiders might find attractive. As such, there is a cycle of growth ultimately funded through the gathering and spending of property taxes. Much like a private firm, municipalities will do what they can to enhance this local "wealth," with other municipalities seen as competing firms (Schneider 1989).

Certain policy areas are more naturally competitive than others, in that they provide more of a specialized than a generalized benefit to one community. These types of policy and service areas help municipalities expand and ultimately achieve gains in the three categories mentioned above. Table 3.3 summarizes these policy areas.

All policy areas could provide a municipal government with a competitive advantage, but it is possible to sort policy areas across a spectrum, from low to high competition. In Table 3.3, policies are grouped along the same lines in which they were measured in the previous chapter. As one would suspect, municipalities are more likely to cooperate on policy items in the low-competition categories. As such, we see agreements reached in these policy areas with higher frequency.

The high-competition category includes public transportation, planning, economic development, recreation, water and sewage, and boundary changes. The rationale for each differs, but the guiding logic behind resisting cooperation in these policy areas is that another community might be unduly enriched through common investment. In other words, one community might receive a competitive advantage through cooperation, which creates general disincentives towards cooperation.

Many of these policy areas address the enhancement of key city services – that is, services that could sway outsiders to locate within a community. For example, a city's transit network might influence the decision to move to one community over another, especially if one community is burdened by heavy congestion and has a limited or inefficient transit system. Public transit typically is seen as providing more of a competitive advantage than roads. The second most frequently cited policy category in the review of interlocal agreements in Chapter 2 was

Table 3.3. Municipal Policy Areas, by Strength of Competition

Characteristics	Competition Strength	
	High	Low
Policy area	• public transportation • planning • economic development • recreation • water and sewage • boundary changes	• emergency services • administrative • animal control • waste • social services • roads
Rationale	• enhancement of key city services • proprietary advantages • possibility to attract business • threat to spatial monopoly	• standardized city services • consistent servicing methods • services for untargeted populations

transportation (see Figure 2.4). As discussed in that chapter, most of these agreements concern such services as road maintenance or snow clearing, and would not be categorized as "high competition." Few of the agreements in the transportation category concern public transit, aside from those found in the Edmonton CMA.

Certain services within this category also have a proprietary advantage, meaning they lead to a high degree of differentiation between communities. Changes in certain services between communities might give one municipality an advantage over another. Again, thinking of public transit, a municipality with higher-order rapid transit might be more attractive than one with a simple bus network. Cooperation within an area such as this might lead to uniformity in service delivery and, thus, a decline in comparative advantage.

Policy areas likely to attract business are also naturally more competitive. An example would be economic development, where cooperation between municipalities is rare, precisely because an effective local economic development strategy could draw businesses from other communities, significantly enriching one community to the detriment of others (Morin and Hanley 2004; Wolfson and Frisken 2000). In that sense, economic development is often seen as a zero-sum game (Goetz and Kayser 1993).

Finally, any policy area that fundamentally threatens a community's territory is likely to be considered "high competition." As Schneider (1989, 14) argues, cities are "spatial monopolists," in that they have a monopoly on the use of a certain amount of land, with which they can attract new residents and flows of capital. Incursions into that territory are generally resisted, which is why we see so little cooperation when it comes to boundary changes and extensions.

In contrast, in "low-competition" policy areas, such as emergency services, municipalities do not perceive a threat to competitive advantage. All municipalities provide such services, which means municipalities need to be largely concerned with meeting the standard of emergency response. Exceeding this level might not bring the same type of competitive advantage as installing higher-order rapid transit. Other policy areas, such as social services, might not be targeted at the types of populations municipalities hope to attract. As discussed above, municipalities aim to attract populations they believe will enhance their community – namely, groups such as business leaders, doctors, lawyers, and those with certain technical skill sets (Lucy and Phillips 2000: Varady and Raffel 1995). Those from lower-income backgrounds might not be as prized by local actors, thereby removing the incentive to enhance social services, as there is no competitive advantage in this area in attracting populations some might see as less desirable.

This is not to say that there are no competitive advantages within these kinds of services. Municipalities might see an advantage in differentiating and enhancing certain services to attract certain types of residents. Policing is a good example. A municipality might have a larger police force or certain specialized equipment in an effort to reduce its crime rate, which potential residents might find attractive. In the end, the perception of low- and high-competition policy areas inevitably rests with individual local actors.

High Competition: Planning and Economic Development

Municipalities covet growth and development. Research has shown that growth provides a municipality status and symbolizes progress (see Duffy 1995; Harvey and Young 2012; Logan and Molotch 1987; Lucy and Phillips 2000). Growth also enhances the local tax base and potentially leads to new jobs and opportunities for residents. It comes as no surprise, then, that municipal actors would compete for growth and development, hoping to bring more of both to their own community.

In the high-competition planning field, an example is the City of London and Middlesex County in Ontario. Middlesex County almost completely surrounds the much more populated City of London. For most of London's history, growth in the area has been directed towards the city. The county, for the most part, has been content to remain rural.[13] In the 1990s, the Town of Middlesex Centre – a lower-tier municipality in Middlesex County – signed an agreement with the City of London to gain access to the city's sewer system, in part because sewage from the community of Arva was polluting nearby Medway Creek (Sher 2012). At this point, the agreement was finalized with London due to fears of environmental contamination. London realized at the time that this arrangement would allow Arva to expand and provide more serviced housing units within the community. In 2000, an amendment to the original agreement limited the amount of residential and commercial development that could be brought onto the sewer system. Commercial access was restricted to 1,000 square metres of new commercial floor space in any given year, without exceeding 4,500 square metres over a ten-year period (City of London and Middlesex Centre 2000).

In February 2011, London City Council received a plan calling for London to expand Arva's access to the city's sewer system in order to facilitate growth (Spicer 2016a). Those in Middlesex Centre hoped that expanded access to London's sewer system could allow the area to grow from 550 to 1,547 residents during the next two decades (Maloney 2011). The request was met with mixed reviews in London. Certain city councillors chastised the plan, arguing that expanding Arva's access would cost the city an estimated $45 million in assessment, while others described the plan as "innovative" and a way to manage growth (Maloney 2011). Ultimately, the City of London rejected the request in the hope of ensuring area growth directed towards the city, not the county. In response, Middlesex Centre revised its growth projections for the area, designating it (and another similar area along London's eastern border) as "urban growth areas," laying out plans to add hundreds of new homes to the area. London officials expressed concerns about the plan and delivered a letter urging the town to reconsider its plans (Van Brenk 2011). Middlesex Centre politicians argued that London officials had "overstepped their boundaries" (Spicer 2016a, 88).

London and Middlesex Centre share a border with very close settlement areas. Just across the border on London's northern edge, residents in Middlesex Centre pay much lower property taxes but live a short drive from many of London's most popular amenities and places of business. London politicians viewed growth over their border as the result of their success. In the view of London officials, development in Middlesex Centre belonged within London's borders and contributing to the city's assessment base. As such, concerns about growth blurred thinking about cooperation and led to a chill in the relationship between the two governments.

Economic development is another high-competition policy area. Staying close geographically to the planning example, a marketing alliance was built around the City of London, Ontario, and purposely excludes the city, hoping to compete directly against it. The Southern Ontario Marketing Alliance (SOMA) has six members: Ingersoll, Perth County, St Thomas, Stratford, Tillsonburg, and Woodstock.[14] Each is a medium-sized city in the region (Perth County is an upper-tier government). SOMA was created to market the region and bring new business and jobs to each of its members. The alliance was designed to compete with larger regional actors, such as London. In a sense, SOMA is intended to level the playing field, providing smaller regional actors with a platform to attract international firms at the same rate as larger municipalities.

In a study of economic development alliances, this author found that the impetus for SOMA's creation was the disproportionate size of London and a fear that the inclusion of London would harm the rest of the collective. One member of SOMA argued that, "we compete with London, working with them isn't in our best interest – they'd take a lot of investment off our plates" (Spicer 2015b, 558). In this case, economic development has created a two-directional effect. On the one side, it has reduced the motivation of smaller regional actors to work with larger ones. In this case, London, Ontario, is seen as competition as much as large international cities such as New York City or London, England. On the other hand, scale does not allow these smaller municipalities to compete directly with cities like London, Ontario. Instead, it prompts strategic cooperation among similarly sized municipal actors.

Low Competition: Emergency Services and Administration

In Ontario's Parry Sound District are two small municipalities named the Township of Carling and the Township of The Archipelago. Combined they have fewer than 2,500 residents (Carling has a population of 1,248 and The Archipelago 556). Since 2009, the two municipalities have shared a senior administrative team. When Carling's clerk-administrator retired, the Township had a difficult time finding a suitable replacement (KPMG 2013). The Archipelago stepped in and approached Carling's mayor with a proposal to share a chief administrative officer (CAO), which Carling's council later approved (KPMG 2013). In 2010, Carling and The Archipelago also began sharing a treasurer after Carling's long-serving treasurer retired (KPMG 2013). According to the agreement between the townships, 60 per cent of the CAO's time is spent at The Archipelago's office and the remaining time in the workweek at Carling's municipal office, while the treasurer is able to work from either office. The salary for the CAO is divided based upon the time spent in each municipality, while the treasurer's salary is shared based upon the number of hours worked for each municipal administration.

Carling and The Archipelago are small municipalities, meaning each experiences challenges with capacity. Sharing a senior administrative team allows both municipalities to free up funds to spend on policy areas that do provide a competitive advantage for their communities. For example, the funds used for a CAO or treasurer – two positions that the public rarely sees or that can provide much of a competitive advantage, given their low visibility – could be used for something like tourism or economic development.

The same sort of logic is present with emergency services agreements. Most municipalities have some type or arrangement to ensure continuity in emergency services, usually fire services. Provincial legislation normally requires such continuity, so some type of contractual arrangement or mutual-aid agreement makes sense to many municipal administrations. An example is a 2007 fire services agreement between the Rural Municipality of Blucher and the City of Saskatoon, Saskatchewan. In the arrangement, Saskatoon provides firefighting, dangerous goods response services, and rescue services to Blucher. In exchange, Blucher agreed to a "pay-for-service" arrangement, whereby the municipality pays $450.00 per hour per equipment response (such as a pumper engine or rescue apparatus). The decision to respond to an emergency is at the discretion of Saskatoon, and once the city responds, Blucher receives an invoice. If for some reason Blucher refused or was unable to pay, Saskatoon is able to terminate the agreement.

In these situations, the logic behind cooperating on fire services is the same as cooperation in administrative services: it frees up resources for policy areas that provide municipalities with a local competitive advantage. Blucher is much smaller than Saskatoon, and, like many other small municipalities, is faced with capacity issues. Emergency services is one policy area that residents, they hope, do not often require. Residents, therefore, expect emergency services to be available, but they are not in a position to evaluate the performance of such services regularly, making cooperation in this area a much more frequent phenomenon. Signing an agreement with Saskatoon for fire services allows Blucher to invest in other policy areas that could provide the community with a local competitive advantage.

Competition between municipalities in metropolitan areas is not total. As Lucy and Phillips argue, "in contrast with most games and war, in local governments strategic planners are not trying to vanquish their opponents ... instead they want to attract a reasonable share of a metropolitan area's value actors and their assets" (2000, 16). An all-or-nothing attitude towards competition leaves no room for cooperation, be it strategic or not. From the previous chapter, it is clear that cooperation is occurring within Canada's metropolitan areas. This competition, however, is strategic and mediated. It is intended to enhance local position and promote growth, but municipalities do not see others intrinsically as enemies in this process. Strategy, therefore, is being employed.

Above, I presented a simple dichotomy between low- and high-competition policy areas. It is easier to reach agreement and cooperate in low-competition policy areas, where competitive advantage is not at stake, than in high. Municipalities sometimes do cooperate, however, in high-competition policy areas. For example, Toronto and York Region have an agreement concerning water services.[15] The agreement dates back to 1974 and establishes a framework where Toronto procures and distributes water to York Region on the basis of pre-established requirements (including a cap on the daily water volume that is transferred) (Spicer 2014).[16] The agreement stemmed from recognition that the Toronto region was growing, and water was needed to sustain development beyond the city's northern border.

At the time, York Region was mostly a growing suburban community, but with limited options for water: Lake Simcoe to the north, Lake Ontario to the south, and local groundwater.[17] Considering the costs and water capacity of local sources and of transporting water from Lake Simcoe, the decision to try to connect to Lake Ontario through Toronto's water network was easy to make. The decision was also eagerly supported by the province, which was originally part of the agreement as a tripartite partner. Considering the province's involvement and the clear capacity need, there was little political opposition to the agreement when it was originally signed. The only major concern came from then-alderman John Sewel, who argued that the agreement would create successive rounds of low-density urban sprawl to the north of the city.

York Region is responsible for contributing to the capital costs of water infrastructure and the expansion of distribution facilities (Spicer 2014). In this case, Toronto has the ability to limit severely York Region's access to water and, therefore, its ability to expand. Every iteration of the agreement has included a hard, but increasing, cap on capacity, ranging from 136 million litres per day when the agreement was originally struck to 440 million litres per day in the 2005 update. The agreement is likely one of the most closely monitored interlocal arrangements in the country. Not only is water usage monitored daily for billing and capacity purposes, but a joint committee also meets four times a year to resolve any issues with the agreement. Within this committee, there are also subcommittees for operations and finance. Beyond this, staff from the operations sections of each municipality's water service communicate almost daily to ensure adequate water supplies. To date, there have been no issues that could not be resolved by the joint committee, the subcommittees, or staff communication.

The attractiveness of communities within York Region would be heavily curtailed if they could not access water, as internal sources are insufficient to supply a region of its size. Cooperation in this area allows York Region to grow, but by placing limits on water transfers Toronto has a mechanism to control this growth. As such, it is not looking for total competition, but mitigated competition. On this level, cooperation makes sense for Toronto. Similar calculations might be conducted by other municipalities considering contracting or cooperating on high-competition policy areas.

Conclusion

Cooperation is challenging and, as seen in this chapter, the decision even to begin a local cooperative relationship is difficult. First, a municipality must establish its needs and wants. Does it make sense to cooperate? What can be gained? Is it better to cooperate than to deliver the service alone? Once the decision is made to explore interlocal cooperation or contracting, a number of conditions need to be established. Any potential partner needs to have similar wants and desires, which is not always a certainty. That potential partner also must have the capacity to cooperate: the staff to devote to exploring and monitoring any potential project and the resources to begin cooperating.

The big decision about local cooperation is strategic: does cooperation hurt or hinder local competitive advantage? As I detailed above, decisions about cooperative advantage are important. Municipalities undoubtedly compete, but this competition is not total. Local actors seek a rightful share of resources (or what they believe is their rightful share). They view other municipalities as potential competition as they seek out population, business, and external resources from the federal and provincial governments. Backed by groupings of local boosters, municipal officials will do what they can to enhance their position. This view of the local "market" affects the type of service and policy areas in which municipalities will consider cooperating or contracting. Certain policy areas are seen as highly competitive, while others are seen as having a low competitive aspect. Ultimately, municipalities employ strategy to determine with whom to cooperate and compete.

Having established how municipalities determine when and with whom to work, the next chapter explores agreement failure and non-cooperation. Once agreements are established, they do not always last. Cooperation is not enduring. Rather, cooperation might be temporary and the result of ongoing strategic thinking about local competitive advantage. How do agreements unravel? What conditions need to be in place to ensure long-term cooperative relationships? What happens when things fall apart?

4 Agreement Failure and Non-cooperation

The preceding chapter explored why municipal governments enter into cooperative and contractual relationships with other municipalities. A number of factors contribute what can be termed the "calculus of cooperation." Simply put, cooperation emerges when the benefits are high and the costs are low. The survey results in Chapter 2 showed that satisfaction with these types of agreements is high; those that have entered into shared service or interlocal contracts are mostly satisfied with the performance of these arrangements. Despite this reported high level of satisfaction, agreements do come to an end. The previous chapter demonstrated that these challenges are not frequent and most might not be fatal, but termination does happen occasionally. Using data from the Ontario Ministry of Municipal Affairs and Housing survey on shared services and information from interviews in several Ontario communities, this chapter discusses the various reasons agreements can fail and partnerships can unravel. I also examine contract management and the methods practitioners use to improve the execution of interlocal agreements.

Agreement and Partnership Failure

Previous chapters discussed the importance of overcoming transaction costs in forming local cooperative agreements. These transaction costs can be broadly sorted into three identifiable types: coordination problems resulting from information deficiencies, negotiation costs derived from dividing mutual gains, and enforcement costs associated with monitoring agreement (Lubell et al. 2002; Maser 1985). We can also add agency costs – the costs of aligning community and political needs in the contracting process. These costs must be low to enter into an agreement and must be kept low throughout its course. Sustaining partnership, however, involves shifting dynamics: agreements are rarely stable over time (Doz 1996). Adding to accruing transaction costs are other factors that play a role in determining the life course and possible termination of an agreement.

The Shifting Nature of Partnership

Agreements are formed with certain expectations, including financial commitments, workload, and resource provision. Over time, the nature of the service area could change, meaning that the commitment level of each partner must also change, which can create stress in the relationship. Where this new commitment greatly outstrips past commitment, the partnership can become strained and the impression created that the relationship is unequal (Narula 1999). Changes in agreements can be expected over time, but articulated goals are important when entering into partnership, which might head off some of the uncertainty later in the relationship. Agreements that are constructed with an eye to the future are likely poised to sustain positive relationships for much longer. For example, an agreement that takes into account changing working conditions, addresses staffing requirements, and includes flexibility in payment schedules can help provide guidance for future actors if unforeseen circumstances place stress on the relationship. Very rigid agreements do not provide such flexibility, and are likely to frustrate working relationships.

Fiscal Stress

Fiscal health is a key driver of decision making in local government. If a municipal government is experiencing poor fiscal health, this can severely limit its ability to deliver new services or pursue new infrastructure projects. Financial strain and poor local economic conditions also might lead to a phenomenon called "service shedding," where a municipality attempts to remove itself entirely from the production and delivery of a particular service (DeLeon 1983; Graddy and Ye 2008; Kodrzycki 1998). As Lamonth and Lamonth (2016, 360) argue, "when governments suffer financial strains due to softening revenues or mounting obligations, they feel pressure to cut back and possibly jettison noncore functions as a way to deal with the problem." It is possible that such fiscal pressure could motivate actors to seek out alternative service delivery means, such as increased interlocal or private contracting, but research has shown that municipalities do attempt to extricate themselves from these obligations at times as well (Kordrzycki 1998;

Lamonthe and Lamonthe 2016; Lewis 2002). Much of this research is American, meaning that some municipalities within that jurisdictional context have much more freedom simply to stop delivering services, but fiscal stress certainly could be a significant driver of contract termination in Canada as well.

Changes in Competitive Dynamics

As mentioned in the previous chapter, competition between local governments is strategic, and directed at achieving a local advantage and enhancing the profile and reputation of the community. The perception of friend and foe can be temporary. Municipalities might shift their view of which local governments pose a competitive threat and which do not. This shift might come during the course of a partnership, and be especially pronounced if one government views the gains of partnership as uneven. If another municipality is being enriched with the local resources of another, it is possible a municipality might opt to cancel an arrangement or increasingly view it negatively over time.

Managing Social Relations

A great deal of research has found that social networks and patterns of interaction are vital in reaching and maintaining interlocal agreements (see Carr, LeRoux, and Shrestha 2009; Feiock, Steinacker, and Park 2009; Shrestha and Feiock 2009). Ongoing patterns of communication among public officials not only help governments identify new opportunities to cooperate, but also help to build trust and familiarity, ultimately converting a metropolitan area into a type of social network (Gulati and Gargiulo 1999; Thurmaier and Wood 2002). Maintaining these ties can enhance a local relationship by facilitating mutual reciprocity (Coleman 1988). Alternatively, relationships that lack these qualities can have the opposite effect: a lack of communication can lead to a lack of trust and, as a result, a lack of cooperation. If a relationship is positive, but devolves over time, partnerships can splinter and agreements can fail. This can involve either a slow disengagement from the other municipality or swift interpersonal conflict among politicians or administrators. Personalities sometimes clash and once-positive relationships can end. Alternatively, a new set of actors – a new council or new senior administrators – might change existing relationships by not engaging as fully as previous actors or by holding other local priorities that do not include the agreement's service areas.

Interorganizational Trust

As mentioned above, trust is an important component in any cooperative relationship. Trust makes the forming of this type of relationship much easier. Simply put, we want to work with those we trust. A healthy degree of trust between two (or more) partners also decreases the cost of monitoring interlocal agreements. The converse is also true, of course: a lack of trust can lead to the unravelling of an agreement. An interesting aspect, however, is trust at different levels of an organization. Hatley, Elling, and Carr (2015) provide a detailed case study of a failed attempt to establish a fire authority in the Detroit, Michigan, area. They found that a lack of trust was a contributing factor for the arrangement's failure. Although there was a degree of trust between politicians and administrators, this did not carry through to front-line fire and emergency services personnel. They found that individual rank-and-file employees did not trust their counterparts, and their representative unions refused to work with the city to draft joint labour contracts because of a fear they would lose the ability to negotiate higher wages collectively at a later date (Hatley, Elling, and Carr 2015). A degree of trust might exist at the top of two (or more) organizations, but if this does not carry through the entire organization, including those who are actually responsible for delivering the service, the agreement could end in failure.

Ideological Shifts

Both the execution and termination of interlocal relationships are highly political (Daniels 1997; DeLeon 1983; Frantz 1997). If an agreement lacks political support, it is unlikely ever to see implementation. But political shifts during the execution of an agreement also might affect its fate (Cameron 1978; Daniels 1995; Kirkpatrick, Lester, and Peterson 1999). Interlocal agreements are not static, and even though the costs of terminating an agreement are high (an aspect discussed in more detail below), a new council or a number of new council members could push for early termination based upon ideology. For instance, past research (Lewis 2002) has found that conservative governments are more likely to terminate services or consolidate departments, mostly stemming from an effort to control cost and reduce the size of government. Similar forces could be exerted within local government, where ideological leanings could force an examination and ultimately the termination of certain interlocal agreements.

Changing Public Opinion

Any interlocal arrangement requires public support (Bozeman 2007; Zeemering 2015). Local politicians who enter agreements that lack the approval of voters run the risk of losing electoral support. Similarly, local administrators who enter agreements without public support risk losing public confidence, which also might have severe personal consequences. For the most part, public knowledge of interlocal agreements is low (Sancton, James, and Ramsay 2000), but residents might be acutely aware of the quality of local services. In fact, some services receive more scrutiny than others. Existing research has found that fire service and protection are areas where the public is cautious about losing control or input to another community (Bickers 2005; Ferris 1986). In such cases, a potential loss of control over service production might be so strong that the net gains of partnership would have to be substantial (Morgan and Hirlinger 1991). Similarly, if service levels were to decline in any policy area, local politicians and administrators would certainly face criticism from the public. The condition of the service matters, making agreement monitoring all the more important. Research on public attitudes towards local cooperation and service sharing in western Europe has shown that interlocal cooperation tends to be supported by voters of progressive left-wing parties but opposed by right-wing nationalist partisans, who tend to favour local autonomy (Strebel and Kubler 2021). In general, if local actors believe that public opinion about and support for a particular shared service have shifted, this might cause them to reconsider its ongoing value.

Explaining Non-cooperation

Above are some general reasons agreements can fail, but I turn now to the experiences of practitioners and real-world examples of agreements that have failed. The data below are from the survey by the Ontario Ministry of Municipal Affairs and Housing conducted by phone in November 2012. Every municipality in the province (444 at the time) was contacted. Of those contacted, 409 responded (a 92.1 per cent response rate). Of those municipalities that responded, 109 reported having some type of agreement failure – 26.6 per cent of survey respondents. This suggests that agreement failure is common, but not frequent.

Information gained from personal interviews with municipal staff and politicians is integrated throughout the section. The Ontario survey allowed the author to identify municipalities that had a failed agreement at some point in its recent history. Each municipality that indicated a failed agreement in the provincial survey was contacted and asked to participate. Seven of these municipalities agreed to be part of an in-depth interview: Port Hope, Charlton and Dack, Parry Sound, Head, Clara and Maria, Essa, Gananoque, and Deep River.[1] These interviews were conducted in July and August 2016.

The other municipalities that were contacted did not participate for a variety of reasons. In some cases, requests for an interview were simply not returned. In others, details of the agreement failure were not readily available. Some administrators refused to discuss details of the agreement's termination for legal reasons (if the termination might find its way to court at some point) or did not want to disclose details in case doing so might sour their relationship with the other party or put current or future cooperative arrangements in jeopardy. In some cases, the only individuals with information about the termination had left the organization or the termination had occurred such a long time ago that the details surrounding the event had been lost. In any case, the author is thankful to those in the participating communities who were able to assist in providing more information about agreement termination.

Figure 4.1 presents the reasons for agreement failure as revealed by the province-wide survey. Of the 109 municipal governments that noted they had experienced an agreement failure of some kind, 7 neglected to provide a reason for the breakdown of the arrangement and were thus excluded. The reasons provided were aggregated into seven broad categories stemming from existing literature on interlocal cooperation: partner disagreement, increase in resources, poor results, capacity issues, a lack of political will, personnel issues, and changes in provincial regulation.

By far, the most frequent rationale for agreement failure is partner disagreement. The categories are quite broad, but this one in particular captures a great deal of activity. Included in this category are generalized disagreements between partners, personnel conflicts, differences in opinion over the course or trajectory of the agreement, or even decisions made to change the agreement based on new perceptions of interlocal competition. In short, agreements can unravel quickly if partners do not see eye-to-eye on certain issues. Many agreements have procedures to work through challenges, including arbitration measures, but even with institutionalized components to avoid disagreement, partnerships can break down.

As an example, Hamilton Township and Port Hope, Ontario, terminated a long-standing agreement to share the Vincent Massey Memorial Centre, a large recreation complex and community centre in Hamilton Township, located close to the border of both communities. The facility was constructed in the early 1970s. The agreement proved

Figure 4.1. Reasons for Agreement Failure

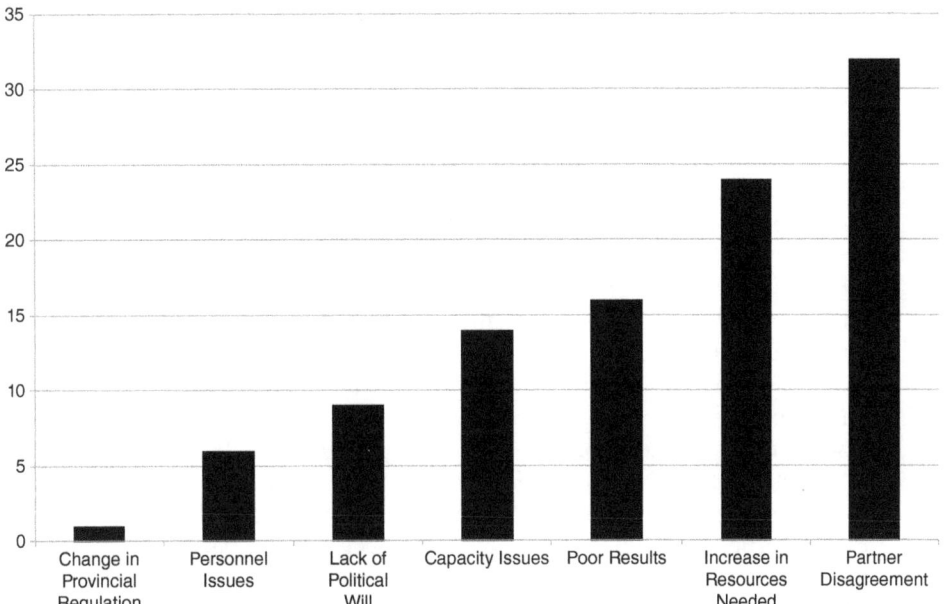

Source: Author's compilation, from Ontario Ministry of Municipal Affairs and Housing Survey, November 2012.

to be quite resilient over time, even surviving a local amalgamation that saw Hope Township and Port Hope consolidated in 2001. After amalgamation, the new municipality inherited the agreement, and opted for it to continue. Hamilton Township managed the facility and Port Hope provided a financial contribution. As a result, residents from both communities received access.

From the author's interview with a Port Hope official in August 2016, the following sequence of events seems to have occurred. In 2006, Hamilton Township applied for a federal grant to upgrade the facility, but did not tell Port Hope, even though the funding agreement required one-third funding from municipal partners.[2] From this point, the relationship between the two municipalities disintegrated, with those in Port Hope feeling they were left as junior partners in the agreement. Many also felt that Hamilton Township ought to have consulted with Port Hope before committing them to financing a facility upgrade. Many in Port Hope's administration and members of council began to question the ongoing viability of the existing arrangement.

Port Hope also did not have any staff on the facility's management board, which led many to question the municipality's ability to influence operations and future expansion. After conducting an analysis of usage, Port Hope concluded that too few of its community members were using the facility to justify paying 50 per cent of the yearly operating costs. Additionally, new regional facilities had been constructed that would be more useful for residents, as well as an existing sports complex within the town that had many of the same facilities, including an ice rink.[3] With the facility's deficit growing and no way to influence decision making on the board, Port Hope council made the decision to terminate the agreement and redirect its share of the cost to other recreation facilities. The town eventually opted to renovate the Jack Burger Sports Complex in 2015, making the facility fully accessible, updating the pools and changing rooms and increasing space available for customer service.

In an effort to keep Port Hope in the agreement, the facility's board of directors offered to reduce Port Hope's yearly contribution, but because the offer did not include representation on the board, the municipality turned it down. By this point, the decision had been made and the chances of reconciliation had passed. Hamilton Township's funding application served as a catalyst to examine an agreement that many had taken for granted for years. Inertia had propelled the agreement forward, but this focusing event led many to seriously question the benefits the community was realizing through partnership. Once a rift had become visible, it was far too challenging to heal. Port Hope officials felt they had been taken advantage of both in the current context and historically. Since the board refused changes, the agreement was no longer palatable.

Returning to the provincial survey, the second most frequently reported category for agreement failure was a need for increased resources. As described above, the conditions under which an agreement is carried out can be very different from those under which it was originally struck. This category captures all those types of arrangements where an increase in financial or material resources required to execute the agreement increased over time to the point where one partner came to see the arrangement as untenable. For example, an agreement could have been created to share a particular piece of equipment between two municipalities but if the operating costs and ongoing transaction costs of the arrangement become too high, it might have made sense for one municipality to purchase and operate its own equipment. This is a very simple example, but one that perhaps illustrates how a change in resources can make an agreement unworkable over time.

Again, an interview by the author with an official of the northern Ontario municipality of Charlton and Dack provides an example of how a change in resources can lead to an agreement's termination. Under a long-standing agreement, residents of Charlton and Dack had access to the resources at the library in the neighbouring municipality of Englehart. Much like the situation between Hamilton Township and Port Hope, the agreement had been in force for many years without any significant changes. Eventually, however, Englehart wanted to move to a new billing model whereby Charlton and Dack would pay $40 per household to continue blanket access to the library facilities, which was equivalent to paying for an individual membership for each resident.

This policy change led Charlton and Dack administrators to explore other options, and eventually terminated the agreement with Englehart in favour of one with the adjacent town of Armstrong. The library in Armstrong, however, proved too far away for many members of the community to use: Charlton and Dack is approximately 20 kilometres from Armstrong, but only five from Englehart. In response, Charlton and Dack officials decided to return to an agreement with Englehart – an improved one, in fact, as Charlton and Dack now has one seat on the library board, allowing the community to have some say over the library's operations.

The next most frequently cited category in the 2012 provincial survey was "poor results." In this category were agreements that failed because outcomes simply did not match expectations. The quality of the service provided might have been too low or the price too high, leading local administrators to believe terminating the agreement would be in their best interest. Again, the alternative in this category would be for a municipality to deliver the service alone in the hope of improving quality or lowering costs. The private sector can be an alternative, but the example of Charlton and Dack and Englehart shows that there is not a private sector alternative for every service.

An example of an agreement that falls into this category is a tourism information office that, at one time, was operated jointly by the municipalities in Parry Sound District, a census division consisting of twenty-two municipalities in northern Ontario. From the author's interview with a Parry Sound official, it appears that, although the agreement had existed for some time, the land on which the tourism office sat was purchased by a private developer, leading some municipalities to believe the office was not delivering additional tourism to their communities. The push to end the agreement came from the Township of McKellar, which had resisted any collaborative tourism efforts from the beginning. Over time, more partners left the agreement. All that is left today are sets of tourism pamphlets sitting inside a private rest stop.

Tourism can be an exceptionally hard service to quantify. Most municipalities do not have an accurate way of tracking visitors, and even if they do, it is difficult to isolate specific efforts as a factor in any change. As such, the shared tourism office was hard to justify, especially given that smaller municipalities such as McKellar did not have the capacity to monitor the impact of the office. Once a private developer purchased the land, confidence in the initiative waned, and partners who were always critical of the office found an opening to end the project.

Two further examples highlight the effect of the perception of agreement performance. The first comes from the author's interview with an official from the United Townships of Head, Clara and Maria, in northern Ontario. An economic development agreement once existed between Head, Clara and Maria and the Towns of Deep River and Laurentian Hills, which essentially called for one staff person from Deep River to provide economic development services for the three communities. Over time, officials in Head, Clara and Maria believed the focus of the partnership was on business and housing development in Deep River and Laurentian Hills, with little return on investment for Head, Clara and Maria. Concerns from staff members in Head, Clara and Maria were disregarded by the other communities, leading Head, Clara and Maria officials to terminate the agreement and contract out economic development efforts.

The second example comes from the author's interview with an official from the Township of Essa, in Simcoe County. Essa had signed an economic development agreement with its neighbouring municipalities in Simcoe County: Innisfil, Bradford, West Gwillimbury, and New Tecumseth. Over time, Essa officials came to believe economic development opportunities were being directed towards the other, larger, municipalities in the partnership. As a result, Essa terminated the agreement and established its own economic development committee, which works in conjunction with Simcoe County's economic development office.

Much like tourism, the results of economic development efforts are difficult to isolate and quantify. Most municipal actors believe some economic development efforts are needed, but, as existing research has shown, competition between municipalities is high when it comes to this policy area (Batrik 1991; Eisinger 1989; Isserman 1994; Meder and Leckrone 2002). As a result, cooperative efforts in local economic development need to overperform. The arrangements in Head, Clara and Maria and in Essa did not do so. With multiple actors involved, the distribution of gains in these types of partnerships needs to be seen as equitable. Arguing that each partner benefits from regional economic performance is usually insufficient (Spicer 2015b). By not overdelivering, these agreements were perceived as underwhelming and perhaps even harmful, given that each municipality was making a financial contribution that was enriching neighbouring communities.

The next most cited category for agreement failure in the 2012 provincial survey was "capacity issues." At certain points, when an agreement is signed, partners might believe they are able to enter into an arrangement and pay for, produce, or deliver a service, either jointly or on behalf of another municipality. Over time, one partner might realize that it does not have the capacity after all to uphold its end of the arrangement, or perhaps no longer has the resources to provide the service. In any case, capacity is not only required to enter into an arrangement, but also to maintain it over time. This category of agreements falls victim to shifting and failing capacity issues.

The categories that follow, "lack of political will" and "personnel issues," include all types of political and administrative issues that might lead to agreement failure. For example, a newly elected council might re-evaluate an agreement and decide that it no longer provides the municipality with value, even if the agreement still has administrative support. An example, from the author's interview with an official from the eastern Ontario municipality of Gananoque, involves an agreement the municipality had with the Township of Leeds and Grenville to share the costs to operate an arena. Gananoque council determined that the cost-sharing formula did not benefit the municipality, and was adamant that a portion of the capital costs be included in the formula. Leeds and Grenville council was just as adamant that it should not have to pay any capital costs, which led to a deadlock as both sets of local politicians refused to back down. After the next election, two new councils were in place, and the municipalities negotiated a cost-sharing formula that did not include capital costs. In exchange, Leeds and Grenville agreed to an even split of the operating deficit. In this case, a change of political will prompted a renewed effort to find agreement.[4]

"Personnel issues" includes human resource issues – for example, if the staff member responsible for executing an arrangement no longer wishes to continue to do so. In some cases, a certain staff member, usually a clerk or a member of legal staff, was shared between municipalities, but no longer wanted to have dual responsibilities. In other cases, the individual involved left or retired.

The eastern Ontario town of Deep River had an agreement in place for many years to share an economic development office with nearby Laurentian Hills. From the author's interview with a Deep River official, it appears that, after the individual who staffed the office retired, it was decided to dismantle the department and transfer responsibility for economic development to Renfrew County – an upper-tier government covering both municipalities – thus saving both municipalities the cost of a new economic development officer. In this case, the retirement forced a re-evaluation of the agreement and an exploration of alternatives. The agreement was terminated, but it did give way to a new arrangement with the county.

The final, and most sparsely populated category of reasons for agreement failure in the 2012 Ontario survey is labelled simply "change in provincial legislation." Only one agreement fell into this category: a service that was shared between two municipalities but split separately by changes in provincial requirements. The municipality in question was not able to participate in an interview, but in the 2012 survey indicated only that the service "did not meet the requirements of the Act." Unfortunately, it is impossible to elaborate on this response, but I discuss the role of provincial authority in dictating the course of interlocal activity in the following chapter.

Figure 4.2 provides an indication of the types of policy areas that were in failed agreements according to the 2012 Ontario survey. Only one respondent failed to indicate what type of service was being shared in the agreement that eventually failed. The same broad categories used in Chapter 2 to record the frequency of agreements are used below.

Most of the failed agreements in the survey can be labelled as "administrative." This usually involves the sharing of staff, which can contribute to failure if there is some type of personnel conflict or human resources dispute. Changes in duties or retirements can lead municipalities to explore the long-term viability of agreements and to readjusting their delivery strategy. In the previous chapter, administrative services were labelled low-competition areas, which remains true here, but because of the personnel issues required in such arrangements, they are prone to failure. Many of the policy areas deemed high competition are represented in Figure 4.2 – especially transportation, planning, water and sewage, recreation, and economic development. In these areas, municipalities naturally see a competitive advantage; as such, cooperation is less likely. What can be added to this conclusion is that when we do see cooperation in these areas, it is susceptible to a higher frequency of failure, which might relate back to the survey response and case studies presented above: resources levels might shift over time, those involved might have fundamental disagreements about the course of the arrangement, capacity problems might emerge, or political will might change.

Figure 4.2. Policy Areas Connected to Agreement Failure

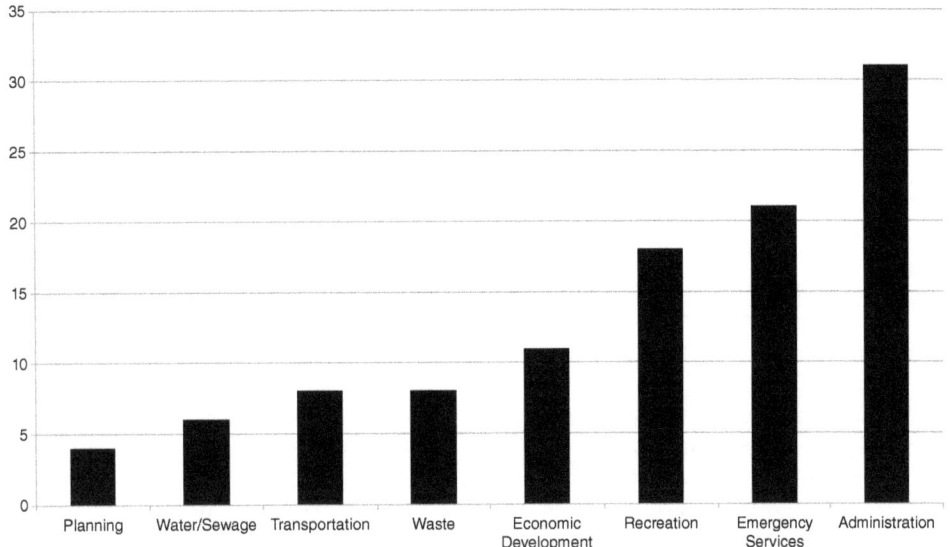

Source: Author's compilation, from Ontario Ministry of Municipal Affairs and Housing Survey, November 2012.

Terminating an Agreement: Determining Costs and Risk

Once a municipal government determines that an arrangement is unworkable or no longer palatable, there are a number of ways to terminate it. Most agreements have conditions outlining when and how that can be done. In most cases, there is a specified period of time – usually at least six months – in which notice of termination must be given. Notice of the termination is usually required in writing. Most agreements contain some kind of language about compensation. If proper termination procedures are followed, there is generally no financial compensation necessary. If, for some reason, the termination does not follow proper contractual procedures, the party pursuing termination may be subject to legal action.

Aside from termination procedures, there are often expiry clauses, where the agreement merely expires at after set period, such as 12 or 24 months. There is usually some information about possible renewal, whereby the partners may extend the agreement for another set period. The agreement also might have an expiry clause or provide for automatic renewal for another set period. A partner that is unsatisfied with the arrangement thus might choose not to renew the agreement or simply wait for it to expire.

Some arrangements take quite a while to exit. For example, it took Port Hope close to two years to terminate fully its participation in the Vincent Massey Memorial Centre. The exit was somewhat unusual, given the length of time – close to forty years – that the municipality had been involved in the arrangement. Port Hope officials entertained offers from the facility's board to keep the municipality from leaving; ultimately, however, the agreement took long to terminate because it had to be unravelled and the contribution of both municipalities examined within a long-term context.

Terminating an agreement is certainly not painless. A variety of costs accompany termination of a contract, such as financial costs, damage to existing relationships, and effects on organizational reputation. In such cases, municipalities must decide if the benefits outstrip the costs.

Financial costs: For most municipalities, the financial strain of partnership is top of mind when considering terminating an agreement. If the municipality is losing money or if administrators find that the service could be delivered at a lower cost by the municipality alone, then a cost-benefit analysis is conducted: do the financial costs of remaining in the agreement outstrip the costs – for example, penalties for early termination – of leaving? If so, then exit is the best option.

Social capital costs: Aside from immediate financial costs, backing out of an intermunicipal agreement can cause disruptions and harm relationships with the other partners. For example, if two municipalities had come together to build a recreation facility, the termination of the agreement by one partner would result in significantly increased costs for the other, considering that the facility likely would have been built to accommodate residents from both communities. Such as termination could lead to less cooperation and even a long-term freeze in interaction between local actors.

Reputational costs: Terminating an agreement might affect the municipality's reputation with other municipalities by signalling that its administration is unstable or unable to commit to long-term relationships, which could lead other municipalities to refuse to enter into agreements with such a municipal government. Municipalities want to project an image of openness and trust, which could be damaged when terminating an agreement, with consequences well into the future.

Municipal actors need to account for all of these costs and consequences when deciding on cancelling an agreement. Could the service be delivered alone at a lower cost? Are there termination fees? Will terminating an agreement sour relationships with local partners? Will such an action reduce the possibility of future cooperation or harm other agreements currently in place? Will termination lead to a negative reputation?

Managing Contracts

Charles Wise (1997, 576) argued that, "in public administration, thus far, more effort has gone into seeking out additional opportunities to contract for services and charting possible cost savings from doing so than has gone into specifying the management imperatives necessary to develop and manage contracts successfully." More than twenty years have passed since Wise's original argument, but very little has changed. Municipalities with interlocal agreements must be aware that this form of service delivery requires maintenance. Whether institutional or social, maintenance comes in a variety of forms, but it is clear that interlocal cooperation and contracting require much more work than in-house delivery. As we have seen in prior chapters, reducing transaction costs can make the execution of these agreements easier and less costly, but municipalities still need to work on their contract-management capacity.

In his seminal book, *Governing by Contract*, Phillip Cooper (2003, 101) argues that "good contract administration is about building and maintaining a positive and effective working relationship that ensures a good deal for the public in the operation of the contract and not just in the selection of a bidder or the drafting of the contract." What Cooper tells us is that ensuring the public receives a "good deal" is an ongoing process. How municipal administrators navigate this process can have serious consequences. Certain factors can help. Romzek and Johnston (2002) argue that contract effectiveness is enhanced when adequate resources are provided for execution, when careful planning occurs for performance measurement, when staffs responsible for contract management receive intensive training, and when contract staff capacity is carefully evaluated.

Again, trust and repeated interaction between administrators and decision makers make contract management easier (Ostrom and Walker 2003; Van Slyke and Hammonds 2003; Yang, Hsieh, and Li 2009). Regular face-to-face meetings are pivotal in avoiding disputes and can swiftly resolve conflict (Ostrom, Gardner, and Walker 1994; Zeemering 2015). Staff and intergovernmental working groups also can be effective in reducing conflict in the right settings, especially if the agreement has multiple actors and crosses a large geographic area (Spicer 2016b; Zeemering 2015).

The structure of contracts themselves matters. The contract should specify clearly what role each government will play and, if possible, which staff person or department will be responsible for the agreement's execution (Brown and Potoski 2006). Financial resources and exchange also should be stated clearly, penalties should be included for failure to adhere to components of the agreement, and there should be regular evaluation periods – preferably by an outside auditor or group. As I have argued elsewhere (Spicer 2017), the public should be more heavily involved in these agreements and have ample opportunity to access and comment upon their contents.

Overall, municipalities would be well served to pay close attention to agreements once they are signed, and take a more proactive approach to contract management. Cooper (2003) argues that municipalities do not budget adequately for contract capacity and too few public employees have specialized training in contract management. Perhaps problems with certain contracts and negative past experiences could prompt municipal administrators to provide more contract-management training. It should also be noted that local governments report lower levels of monitoring for services provided by other governments than for services provided by private firms, indicating that interlocal contracts might be easier to manage than contracts with the private sector (Marvel and Marvel 2007, 2008)

Conclusion

Intermunicipal agreements are challenging to form; they can be even more challenging to maintain. Despite the high levels of satisfaction revealed in surveys, agreements do fail if municipalities believe the costs outweigh the benefits. The partners might disagree about costs or changes to the agreement or the agreement could simply be producing poor results. If municipal officials determine that an agreement is no longer producing benefits, the next consideration is termination costs, including the harm to local relationships and the municipality's reputation. All of these issues need to be factored into the decision to terminate any interlocal agreement. The result is that municipalities do not often terminate agreements – the majority are formed and end just as they were designed, without negative effects on any of the partners.

5 The Role of the Provinces

In Canada, provincial governments regulate the shape, scope, and function of municipalities. Given the nature of this relationship, it should come as no surprise, then, that provincial governments often affect the course of local cooperation. This brief chapter examines the role of the provinces in either facilitating or impeding local cooperation.

As mentioned earlier in the book, the British North America Act of 1867 established a distribution of powers between the federal and provincial governments that placed the responsibility for municipalities with the provinces. Since, provincial governments have used nearly the full range of their authority not only to impose new service areas upon municipalities, but also to change their borders and consolidate them with neighbouring communities. Provincial governments have also attempted to "disentangle" policy responsibility between provincial and municipal governments (Sancton 2000; Siegel 2005). Part of this has involved "uploading" certain services (such as education) and "downloading" others (such as social services) in an effort to balance service responsibility and financing between provincial and municipal governments (Graham and Phillips 1998). Despite some local opposition and concern regarding assigning local service functions, provincial governments have often made such changes unilaterally with little local input (Spicer 2015b).

Another (frequently used) dimension of provincial authority is the ability to consolidate local governments and adjust municipal boundaries. Canada's largest cities have often engaged in rounds of outward expansion, absorbing vast amounts of suburban and rural territory in the process, all with the blessing of their respective provincial governments. The largest institutional changes, however, came with the creation and subsequent consolidation of regional institutions. In 1953, Ontario passed legislation that created a two-tier structure that would cover Toronto and its surrounding municipalities (Frisken 2007). Known as Metropolitan

Toronto, this new two-tier structure consisted of the City of Toronto and thirteen surrounding suburban municipalities, and was widely praised for balancing regional interests with local representativeness (Kaplan 1965). Metropolitan Toronto was followed by the creation of ten new regional governments, mostly in southern Ontario (Fyfe 1975). In the 1990s and 2000s, many of these regional governments were restructured. In 1998, the provincial government amalgamated Metropolitan Toronto to create a large, single-tier municipality (Frisken 2007). Regional governments in Hamilton-Wentworth, Ottawa-Carleton, and Sudbury followed suit some years later. A similar pattern occurred in Winnipeg, where the Manitoba government created and then subsequently amalgamated a regional government (Higgins 1986; Kiernan and Walker 1983). Large-scale amalgamations have been experienced elsewhere – large cities such as Montreal and Halifax were made even larger by provincial governments that saw fit to combine them with vast swaths of rural and peri-urban territory (Sancton 2001). Arrayed across some of these regions is a variety of coordinating agencies, such as the Capital Region Committee in Winnipeg and the Alberta Central Regional Alliance around Edmonton (Sancton 2011). In all this, municipalities have been virtually powerless to resist these changes. There is nothing akin to "home rule" in Canada (Lightbody 1997). Provincial governments often make complete changes to municipal policy responsibility and structure unilaterally.

A Provincial Role in Local Cooperation

Provincial governments often influence the types of decisions local actors make, mainly due to the authority vested in the provinces over municipal institutions. This includes decisions surrounding interlocal cooperation and service sharing. Provincial governments can limit cooperation between municipalities in a number of ways. The first, of course, is simply to ban service sharing and cooperative activity between municipalities. For instance, a provincial government certainly would be within its right to dictate that service collaboration or contracting between municipalities is strictly off limits. It is hard to find instances where this has occurred in Canada, however, as provincial governments have often been content to allow municipalities to determine their own service levels and standards. Servicing responsibility is certainly something that is generally included in provincial legislation on municipal affairs, but the content of that service is usually assumed to be a municipal responsibility.

Although provincial governments have not been keen to disallow interlocal cooperation and contracting, this is not to say they have not tried to dissuade the practice in the past. In this regard, precedent does exist. In

February 1987, Ontario Minister of Municipal Affairs Bernard Grandmaître convened a panel to examine the province's county system. The minister tasked the committee – headed by MPP Ray Haggerty and composed of three mayors of lower-tier municipalities, two from counties, and one from the Ottawa-Carleton regional government – to examine "retooling and reshaping" the county system, but not restructuring it (Ontario 1987, i). The resulting report – *Patterns for the Future* – focused mainly on the structure of the county system and the viability of small and separated municipalities, but the committee did have a few interesting findings regarding interlocal agreements. These agreements, the committee argued, were a potential source of trouble for municipal policy makers. Noting that interlocal agreements can be "time-consuming to negotiate, can foster dispute, and can create confusion about accountability," the report argued that these agreements create uncertainty about the county's role as a policy maker (Ontario 1987, 62). Furthermore, the report argued that interlocal service sharing causes public uncertainty about which level of government is responsible for which service (65). Interlocal agreements, the report continued, do not necessarily provide stable administration since their terms and conditions are subject to periodic renegotiation, thus detracting from a serious consideration of the county's assumptions of a service (65). Yet, despite its resistance to interlocal agreements, the report recommended that counties continue to be allowed to enter into such agreements (66). As I discuss below, there is significant evidence that the Ontario government no longer views interlocal cooperative agreements in the same light.

Finally, provincial governments may limit interlocal cooperation in a number of implicit ways. For example, we know from past research that larger municipalities tend to have fewer cooperative agreements (Post 2004), partly because of distance and challenges associated with geography. Proximity creates opportunity for collaboration, so when the provincial government creates larger municipalities, it reduces some of the natural opportunities to collaborate (Spicer 2016a). Amalgamation also increases municipal capacity, and therefore the desire to create more servicing in-house. Need and opportunity could be reduced through institutional changes, such as amalgamation or the creation of two-tier regional structures.

Even though provincial governments have the tools effectively to end or limit interlocal contracting and service sharing, most acknowledge the benefits and encourage the practice. There are good reasons for doing so: an increase in interlocal contracting or service sharing might reduce municipal expenditures, but also might take pressure off provincial government to fill servicing gaps, especially in northern and remote communities.

One way to encourage and enhance interlocal cooperation is through flexible institutions. The best example is British Columbia's regional districts, which offer a particularly effective setting for service sharing (Bish 2001). Participation is voluntary,[1] and individual municipalities may opt in or out of every service. Regional district boards consist of members appointed by member municipal councils along with directly elected members from unincorporated areas, providing a venue for discussing intermunicipal cooperation and shared servicing (Cashaback 2001). Regional districts determine which services to deliver to which geographic areas. They do not have the legal ability to impose a tax, but are able to requisition payments from member municipalities to cover services received. Therefore, the financial contribution of each municipality, in theory at least, equals the benefits received.

An example of these regional districts, and one from which agreements for this book's survey were collected, is the Greater Vancouver Regional District (GVRD) – more commonly known as Metro Vancouver. The GVRD consists of twenty-one members: Village of Anmore (population as of 2016 census, 2,092), Village of Belcara (644), Bowen Island Municipality (3,402), City of Burnaby (223,218), City of Coquitlam (126,495), Corporation of Delta (99,868), Electoral Area A (13,035), City of Langley (25,081), Township of Langley (104,743), Village of Lion's Bay (1,318), City of Maple Ridge (76,052), City of New Westminster (65,976), City of North Vancouver (48,770), District of North Vancouver (86,396), City of Pitt Meadows (17,965), City of Port Coquitlam (56,347), City of Port Moody (32,975), City of Richmond (190,473), City of Surrey (468,359), Tsawwassen First Nation (720), City of Vancouver (605,071), District of West Vancouver (44,989), City of White Rock (19,339), and City of Abbotsford (133,765).[2] As is clear from the membership list, the GVRD includes both large and small members – in terms of both geography and population. Providing policy for such a range of members can be challenging, but, given its flexible nature, the structure is generally well regarded (see Bish 1999, 2002; Bish and McDavid 2016; Cashaback 2001; Spicer and Found 2016; Wolman 2016).

To get a sense of the degree of the service sharing and collaboration within the GVRD, we examined the agreements the GVRD in place with constituent municipalities over the period from 1995 to 2013, the same time frame as in Chapter 2. In total, we found 131 such agreements, most (78 per cent) still in force.[3]

In Chapter 2, we found that the vast majority of sharing or contracting occurs within the area of emergency services (in the form of mutual-aid agreements, fire or police despatch, and so on). Administrative and transportation agreements were the next two most frequently cited areas of cooperation. Unlike the municipalities discussed in Chapter 2,

Figure 5.1. Cooperative Policy Areas, Greater Vancouver Regional District

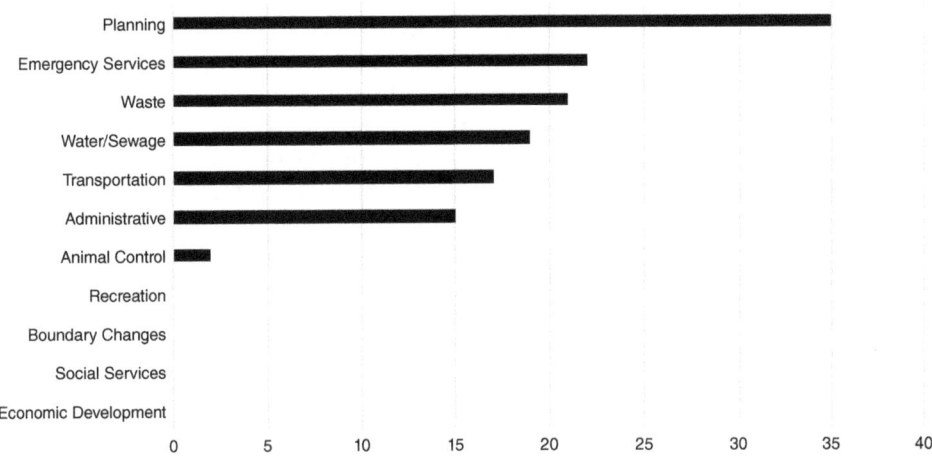

however, the GVRD has a considerable number of agreements in the areas of planning, waste, water and sewage, and transportation (as shown in Figure 5.1). Planning is a "high-cooperation" policy area in that it includes portions of local policy that affect competitive advantage.

There is some support in the literature for the notion that bodies such as the GVRD enhance interlocal cooperation. Bish (1999, 22) argues that "a major advantage of the regional district system has been that regional districts provide a political forum that reduces the cost of negotiating benefiting area agreements, partly because voting rules were fixed and a default financing rule based on converted assessed value was provided." Walisser, Paget, and Dann (2013, 162) similarly argue that "RDs [regional districts] have resolved hundreds of interlocal servicing problems … this is a singular achievement in that, while often encouraged in local government systems worldwide, successful implementation of joint servicing schemes is comparatively rare." In essence, the regional district system works to reduce transaction costs and potentially ensuing conflict (Bish and Clemens 2008, 62).

Overall, the regional district system fosters and encourages cooperation by explicitly structuring upper-tier municipalities as agents for lower-tier partners (Bish 2000). Bish and McDavid (2016, 24) argue that regional districts have a strong role "to provide a form and administrative structure for shared service cooperation so that each service does not have to have a one-of-a-kind arrangement … this appears to lead to greater cooperation and more shared services for mutual benefits than with other kinds of local government structure."

Another avenue for provincial governments hoping to enhance local cooperation is simply to force municipalities to cooperate. Alberta is a recent example of this trend. Amendments to Alberta's Municipal Government Act introduced mandatory agreements for municipalities in the province, including growth management boards in the Edmonton and Calgary regions, mandatory intermunicipal collaboration frameworks (ICFs) that include intermunicipal development plans for all municipalities that are not members of regional growth management bodies. Municipalities that were not members of a growth management board were given two years to prepare and adopt an ICF with each municipality with which they share a boundary (Mertz 2016; Stolte 2016). Those unable to reach agreement would be forced into arbitration.

Time will tell if Alberta's initiative is successful, but history is not on the province's side. Another example is Ontario's experience with its Consolidated Municipal Service Manager (CMSM) program, introduced during a period of service realignment and rounds of "uploading" and "downloading" of services between the provincial government and local governments. The CMSM was a product of the Local Services Realignment Act, introduced in 1998, which essentially transferred responsibility for social assistance, childcare, social housing, land ambulance, and public health to municipalities (Spicer 2015a). In exchange, the provincial government "uploaded" the costs for education. The goals of the CMSM were to provide greater accountability for taxpayers, protect priority services, maintain critical standards, streamline service delivery, rationalize funding responsibilities, capitalize on local expertise, and reduce waste and duplication (Spicer 2015a). The province felt it could achieve these goals by having CMSM services provided by local governments, rather than at the provincial level. In total, the province created thirty-seven consolidated municipal service manager districts and ten northern social service administrative boards, each of which would be roughly aligned with previously existing jurisdictions (Spicer 2015a). Although the province automatically assigned responsibility for CMSM services to most municipalities (upper-tier governments, such as regional, county, or district governments), counties with a separated city were not assigned a service manager, meaning they would have to share the service jointly and come up with acceptable local terms.

When rural and urban municipalities were forced to come to agreement on the funding and delivery of these services, many were unable to find common ground because of distinctions perceived between "urban" and "rural" services. A great deal of resentment about the process resulted, and relationships between a number of municipal actors soured to the point where nearly all communication was halted for years. In essence, forced cooperation led to a decrease – or even the end – of voluntary cooperation (Spicer 2015a).

A third way for provincial governments to enhance interlocal cooperation is by providing the tools to help municipalities cooperate. For example, Ontario, in conjunction with the Municipal Finance Officers Association of Ontario, has produced a guide to help municipalities seeking to share services. The guide paints an optimistic picture of service sharing and cooperation, arguing that "long term, shared services can be an important ingredient in sustaining local services, which contributes to a municipality's overall financial sustainability ... it is worthwhile to invest time to ensure municipal shared services arrangements are operating as effectively and efficiently as possible" (MFOA 2012, 4). To help facilitate this process, the guide provides an overview of the types of agreements in place across the province, and demonstrates how to form intermunicipal agreements and divide costs and responsibilities.[4] Other provincial municipal associations, such as the Alberta Association of Municipal Districts and Counties (2005, 2008), Saskatchewan Parks and Recreation Association (2015), and the Federation of Canadian Municipalities (2011) have produced similar guides for their members.[5]

Provincial governments have also helped provide information to municipalities. For instance, Newfoundland and Labrador, Quebec, and Saskatchewan have produced similar documents and examples for municipalities considering shared-services agreements.[6] One of the most active provincial governments, however, is that of Nova Scotia, which has produced an extensive guide for municipalities hoping to enter into such agreements.[7] The document outlines the process of cooperation, best practices for establishing agreement, considerations for cost estimation, a discussion of spillover effects, case studies, typologies of agreements, basic elements of agreements, and legal advice for mitigating risk. Nova Scotia's efforts even include a downloadable cost-sharing template that provides a means for determining who is using the service and the actual cost of providing and producing the service. The template removes some of the uncertainty about which municipality should bear the larger burden of costs or whether a particular service should be shared evenly from a financial perspective. Overall, the Nova Scotia government believes there are tangible benefits for municipalities to enter into such arrangements: "collaborating with other municipal units to provide services regionally has the potential to increase cost effectiveness and improve or maintain service delivery standards ... service sharing helps municipalities respond to pressures to reduce tax rates and minimize costs while maintaining or improving service levels" (Nova Scotia 2014, 5). The document further argues that interlocal cooperation can prevent the duplication of services, equipment, and facilities, and spread service costs over a larger population.

Overall, provincial governments have taken a number of steps to bring about local cooperation. Mandated cooperation is likely the least effective, as municipalities forced to find agreement are likely to disagree, possibly souring local relationships. In this sense, mandated cooperation might lead to less voluntary cooperation, and thus might be counterproductive. British Columbia's regional districts are an example of a flexible forum in which service sharing can be discussed. Various provincial efforts to encourage participation have also shown promise in helping municipalities reach agreement. It is likely easier to support municipalities hoping to share services and do what is possible to remove barriers to cooperation and reduce competition than forcing shotgun marriages in the hope some relationship blooms.

Conclusion

Provincial governments play a key role in shaping the scope and function of local government in Canada. Municipalities lack the type of protections that certain US cities enjoy, such as home rule. As a result, they have been subject to numerous rounds of consolidation and service downloading. Because of repeated amalgamations and annexations, there are fewer municipal governments in Canadian metropolitan areas than in other countries, particularly the United States. This, of course, is one way that provincial governments have affected the use of interlocal agreements. Amalgamated governments are large entities, with less imperative to sign cooperative agreements with other municipalities.

Provincial governments, however, are starting to see the value of interlocal cooperation. Numerous provincial governments are trumpeting the benefits of intermunicipal agreements, telling municipal leaders they can improve service quality and lower service costs. A number of strategies have been employed to achieve this effect, ranging from forced cooperation to the implementation of flexible regional bodies to encourage service sharing. Although British Columbia's system of regional districts shows promise, mandatory or forced cooperation has been shown to have a detrimental effect on future, voluntary cooperation. A more fruitful strategy appears to be to give municipal governments the tools to cooperate and remove barriers to interlocal cooperation.

6 Conclusion

This book started by asking a long-standing question in urban political science and public administration: how and why do local governments work together? In Canada, we see evidence of interlocal cooperation and contracting for a range of services in various communities of all shapes and sizes. As mentioned in the first chapter, some of these relationships are old, others are new; some are strong, others fragile; some relationships fail and agreements fall apart. What these agreements represent, however, is a desire on the part of certain governments to pursue flexible servicing options. Because of a range of factors, such as geography and fiscal stress, these municipalities are looking for alternatives to traditional service delivery, and willing to experiment and take some risk to reach that goal.

Throughout this book, the case has been made that interlocal cooperation and service sharing deserves more scholarly attention in Canada. As we have seen, some of these agreements govern important services, such as water and transportation, which have an impact on the everyday lives of residents in communities across the country. It is important that we understand and take seriously the mechanics of these agreements. We need to understand what conditions promote cooperation, which hinder the process, and how the governance of these relationships can be improved for those municipalities that choose to pursue this servicing option. This chapter provides a summary of the findings in this book and lays out an agenda for future researchers hoping to delve deeper into the mechanics of local government administration and service delivery in Canada.

Intermunicipal Cooperation in Canada

This project began with two goals: to assess the local cooperative or contracting landscape and to explain the local cooperative or contracting process. Within each dimension, there was a range of research questions. These are presented again, below.

Assessing the local cooperative landscape:

- who is cooperating?
- what services and policy areas are involved?

Explaining the local cooperative process:

- why do municipalities cooperate?
- why do municipalities not cooperate?
- what leads to successful cooperative relationships?
- what leads to agreement failure?
- what roles do the provinces play in this process?

Through document analysis, primary interviews and employing survey data, we can provide some answers to these questions.

Many municipalities cooperate or contract, but do so in a small range of policy areas

For this study, 648 interlocal agreements were collected from twelve Canadian Census Metropolitan Areas, governing a range of services. Most municipalities within these CMAs cooperate to some degree. The most basic type of relationship is information sharing: two municipalities exchanging information about best practices or about certain programs can be classified easily as intermunicipal cooperation. The risks of these types of relationships are low: there is no exchange of money or resources, staff are not greatly affected or distracted from their regular duties, and there is a clear benefit – namely, the promotion of information and best practices for use in service or policy development. When introducing higher-order relationships involving contracting or cooperating in service or policy areas, the dynamics change. Municipalities become concerned about resources, risk, and competition. The benefit is not always clear and, as a result, the cost of cooperation increases. That does not mean, however, that cooperation is impossible, just that it becomes more challenging depending on the service, the term of the arrangement, and the resources involved. These types of relationships did emerge in the sample, but not at a high frequency. The data collection in the sample was supported by the results of two surveys. The first, collected by the Ontario provincial government, found that 92.4 per cent of the municipalities that responded had some type of cooperative or contractual relationship with other local governments. The frequency of these relationships, however, was much lower than one would expect to see in many metropolitan areas around the world, especially in the United States. In Canada, municipalities tend to cooperate and contract less, but there is certainly a range of cooperative activities happening within Canadian local government.

Most of the agreements collected were for emergency, administrative, and transportation services – a finding confirmed by the 2012 provincial survey that was also used for this book. When an "intensity" calculation was applied to the sample, it was found that many of these agreements are of low intensity, meaning they were designed for service and policy areas that are not very costly or vital to municipal operations. In fact, they were mostly designed to mitigate risk, and do not significantly bind the actors together for any type of meaningful term. As such, it would be fair to say that Canadian municipalities cooperate or contract with their peers, but are tepid, risk-averse actors.

With that said, there is indication that interest in interlocal cooperation is increasing. Survey data presented in Chapter 3 showed that most administrators were keen to sign interlocal agreements. Most viewed these arrangements in a positive light, and those who had interlocal agreements in place or had worked in an environment where they were used reported a positive experience, with few challenges. Of course, there is a large difference between thinking positively about interlocal cooperation and contracting and actually signing an interlocal agreement. Getting to the stage of committing to an agreement has proved challenging for many municipal governments in Canada to this point.

Most municipal actors hope to increase efficiency and save money

Chapter 3 examined the motivation to explore signing cooperative and contractual agreements. Existing literature tells us that municipal actors enter into cooperative and shared-services agreements based upon four main factors: fiscal incentives (lowering production, delivery, or capital costs), filling service gaps (delivering a service the municipality was unable to do on its own or overcoming geographic/environmental isolation), increasing service capacity or quality (tapping into external policy knowledge or using external contributions to buy new equipment or delivery mechanisms), and controlling externalities (managing policy spillover, better directing growth and development). A final category is more prevalent in the Canadian context than elsewhere internationally: mandated integration, where provincial governments force two (or more) municipalities to cooperate.

The survey data presented in this book confirm these findings, demonstrating that the top reasons for considering cooperating or contracting with another municipality concern increasing efficiency and lowering service costs. In short, municipal decision makers are looking to deliver higher-quality services at a lower price – a naturally understandable position not only for government administrators looking to maximize their financial resources, but also for political actors seeking to reduce the tax burden on voters. Cooperative relationships are seen as one route to achieve this.

In our 2012 provincial survey, respondents were asked to estimate how much they saved per year from their cooperative relationships. Of the 378 responses from municipalities that had agreements in place, 206 were willing to make an estimate, with 93 placing a dollar value on the yearly savings from their interlocal agreements. The average response was $95,780 a year – which is a significant amount of money, especially if you are an administrator in a small municipality. However, 91 responded that they did not know how much money was being saved, and 22 indicated that costs actually had increased since signing the agreement. What this indicates is that there is at least a powerful perception that these agreements save money, although many administrators were unable to calculate the precise amount of savings, if any.

Intermunicipal cooperation can be difficult

Although the benefits might be clear to many municipal politicians and administrators, forming interlocal agreements is challenging. Existing literature tells us that the prospects for establishing cooperative agreements are partially related to transaction costs. Chapter 1 and 3 reviewed three types of transaction costs: coordination problems resulting from information deficiencies, negotiation costs arising from dividing mutual gains, and enforcement costs associated with monitoring any agreement (Maser 1985). Cooperation between local governments increases when the potential benefits are high and the transaction costs of coordinating, negotiating, monitoring, and enforcing an arrangement are low (Lubell et al. 2002).

The surveys used for this book revealed that the prospects of forming and maintaining interlocal cooperative or contractual agreements often go beyond transaction costs into the realm of political and interpersonal factors, which can greatly affect the decision to work with other local governments. Respondents indicated that the two most important characteristics of a potential partner were a common need – meaning two municipalities share a need to deliver a service or have a common servicing problem they could help to solve together – and a shared border. Need might create opportunity for governments to work together, meaning that anything from a common service challenge, such as poor boundary roads or a need to upgrade a water distribution system, can spark conversation and, perhaps, a cooperative working agenda. A common need also establishes relationships without predetermined power imbalances. Proximity is equally important, as a shared border might put municipal actors into more frequent conversation, which can increase trust and reduce the perception of risk. Chapter 3 also detailed the competitive edge with which local governments view certain policy areas, such as economic development. Cooperation is, therefore, more likely in policy areas that are less competitive and do not directly lead to or diminish a local competitive advantage.

Two additional factors are good fiscal health and trust. Here, municipal administrators and politicians seek stability. Good fiscal health is an indicator of stability, as well as of capacity, meaning that a particular municipality can be a good partner over the course of an agreement. Just as important is trust. Municipal administrators want to work with those they trust. When trust is high, perception of risk is generally low. High levels of trust also reduce the need for monitoring an arrangement, which ultimately lowers the cost of the agreement, leading to potential efficiency gains.

There are limits to cooperation

Municipalities pursue interlocal cooperation for a number reasons: fiscal incentives, filling service gaps, enhancing service capacity and quality, controlling externalities, and a mandate to do so from the province. The most frequent responses from administrators and politicians when asked why they pursue cooperative and contractual relationships were to lower costs and increase efficiency. Local actors essentially are hoping to deliver better services to residents at lower costs.

In Chapter 3, the argument was made that municipalities seek out a local competitive advantage, hoping to draw residents and businesses to their communities. Municipalities are more likely to cooperate in "low-competition" policy areas, such as emergency or administrative services, rather than in "high-competition" policy areas, such as economic development. Policy areas typified by high levels of interlocal cooperation might provide another community a local strategic advantage. Cooperating with another municipality in a high-competition policy area might enrich one community at the expense of the other. This is not to say that cooperation does not take place in high-competition policy areas; rather, that municipalities use strategic decision making when determining whether or not to cooperate.

Reaching the decision to cooperate or contract with another municipality is not easy, and there are a number of reasons a municipality might be hesitant to sign an agreement. Survey data show that political factors play a role in the decision: a divided council and poor fiscal health are the main reasons municipalities avoid cooperating. Municipalities seek stability, especially in policy areas with a large financial commitment, such as infrastructure projects, and political instability and poor fiscal health are fundamental challenges to an agreement. Terminating an agreement comes with a huge cost and risk. If a municipality does not have the resources to support an agreement, the other partner (or partners) might be left with a host of unanticipated costs and liabilities, along with the possibility of diminished service quality for their residents. Avoiding potential risks often means sizing up potential partners prior to entering into any potential agreement.

There are clear reasons some agreements succeed and others fail

For a municipality to enter into a cooperative agreement, there must be some local competitive advantage, a stable partner, a high degree of trust, frequent communication, and low costs of monitoring and enforcing the agreement. The agreement ultimately also must have public support and be politically palatable.

Even in cases where these conditions are met, agreements might not last. The literature has identified several ways in which agreements can unravel: a shift in the dynamics of the partnership (a change in commitment levels, a change in service area, for example), fiscal stress (poor fiscal health, a decline in the tax base), a change in competitive dynamics between partners, poor social relations between municipal actors, a decline in interorganizational trust, ideological shifts among council members in one (or more) municipalities, and a change in public opinion. The survey data identified a number of other reasons agreements collapse, of which the most frequently cited were disagreement between partners, an increase in resources needed, and poor results from the agreement. Primary interviews expanded upon many of these factors, providing an intimate view of how some arrangements simply unravel. The case studies demonstrated that some end acrimoniously, while others, such as the library agreement between Charlton and Dack and Englehart, can be terminated for administrative convenience, only to be resumed after some service experimentation.

Terminating a formal agreement is not a costless enterprise. Simply because an agreement has stopped producing benefits does not mean a municipal government can extricate itself easily from a contractual arrangement. Many agreements clearly spell out how and when they can be terminated, with specific conditions that must be met. Beyond contractual obligations there are other costs, including financial costs in the form of cancellation fees or compensation, social costs stemming from the breakdown of a local relationship, and reputational costs that accrue from the stigma of agreement failure. Given the challenges of terminating a contract, it is unsurprising that municipal actors usually undertake due diligence before entering into any type of contractual or shared services relationship with another government.

Provincial governments have negatively influenced interlocal cooperative arrangements in the past

In Canada, provincial governments hold a great deal of authority over municipalities. As a result, provincial governments heavily influence the nature of interlocal cooperation. Numerous rounds of annexation and amalgamation in nearly every province have created larger municipalities, reducing the number of potential cooperative and contracting partners, while also reducing the need and incentive to pursue interlocal servicing relationships. In the past, some provincial governments – mainly that of Ontario – also tried to dissuade the use of interlocal cooperation, arguing it could foster intergovernmental division and bitterness. These governments believed that any dispute stemming from failed intergovernmental negotiations or servicing relationships would require provincial intervention. Over time, however, these attitudes apparently have changed. Today, most provincial governments acknowledge there are certain benefits to intermunicipal cooperation, and have begun encouraging municipal governments to cooperate to a greater extent. We have seen provincial governments promote interlocal cooperation through flexible regional institutions, such as British Columbia's regional districts, and through information-sharing campaigns, such as Nova Scotia's detailed guides and resources, which are available to municipal actors in that province.

This change in attitude on the part of provincial governments is welcome. Encouraging municipalities to work together could reduce municipal expenditures; it could also take pressure off provincial governments to fill servicing gaps (especially in northern and remote communities) and solve externality problems. In this sense, allowing and encouraging municipalities to solve local servicing dilemmas cooperatively would give provinces greater ability to devote resources elsewhere.

Linking Regions, Linking Functions

This project offers some lessons for municipal practitioners who might want to explore local cooperative or contractual agreements, but perhaps are unsure of how to start. How can a municipality build lasting relationships and coordinate efforts effectively not only to manage externalities, but also to enhance local resources? What leads to successful interlocal partnerships?

Communication: We naturally gravitate towards and want to work with those with whom we are familiar. Frequent meetings and discussions help to foster trust and allow partnerships to grow. Once a mutual need is identified, it is easier to move the cooperative process along if there is a long history of familiarity. Communication can be a proactive step in the cooperative process. Even if there is no immediate desire to build a cooperative relationship, frequent communication can lay the groundwork. Municipalities that isolate themselves are unlikely to forge many positive interlocal relationships and agreements. The interviews conducted for this project indicate that good local servicing relationships tend to begin with building good local personal relationships.

Trust: To work together – especially in policy areas that require a significant transfer of assets or are of high value – municipal actors need to trust one another. In some cases, signing an interlocal agreement is like going into business together. You would not operate a business with someone you did not trust completely. The same is true for interlocal relationships, which trust helps to create and maintain. A high degree of trust also lessens monitoring costs: without such trust, municipalities must devote more resources to ensuring the agreement is followed. The interviews conducted for this project indicate that trust is important, but also that it is a fragile commodity: when trust between two more parties is lost, it is challenging to rebuild and ultimately affects any potential future relationship. A related attribute is reputation: municipal actors and governments can quickly gain a reputation as untrustworthy, which can deter other municipal governments from exploring cooperative or contractual servicing relationships with them.

Capacity: Along with willingness, another major building block for cooperation is capacity. The municipality must have the ability – the equipment, staff, money, and time – necessary to devote to an agreement. Survey work for this book reveals that municipal officials consider capacity to be a key component of the cooperative process, and look actively for partners with that ability, which also helps to achieve a certain degree of comfort with the agreement.

Transparency: Interlocal agreements are not easy to complete, and a degree of secrecy surrounds them. They are public documents; they are just not publicly accessible. That is not only a problem for researchers and the public; it also limits potential cooperation between municipalities. Ready access to the experiences of other municipal governments would benefit municipal officials who are considering entering into an interlocal agreement. Broader sharing would also facilitate best practices in agreement formation.

Good fiscal health: Tied very closely to capacity is good fiscal health. The survey research for this book reveals that municipalities value good fiscal health in a potential partner. Capacity speaks to the basic means of cooperation, but good fiscal health goes one step beyond and indicates to municipalities that a potential partner has more than just basic resources. It also signals a track record of fiscal prudence and an attention to costs for service production and delivery – both highly desirable traits.

Low-competition policy areas: Chapter 3 made a distinction between high- and low-competition policy areas. The argument was made that municipalities are more likely to cooperate in low-competition policy areas, such as administrative or emergency services. These types of policy areas provide little to no local competitive advantage, especially compared to the policy areas classified as high competition – such as public transit or economic development. Simply put, a higher-order transit system or a robust local economy is more likely to produce the resources that are highly sought after by municipalities, such as new residents and businesses.

Public support: Municipalities need the support of the public for any agreements they sign. This is often referred to in the literature as "agency costs." If an agreement loses public support, it is likely to be terminated. For example, Chapter 3 explored an innovative local agreement that saw the Townships of Carling and The Archipelago in Ontario share a senior administrative team. The agreement was terminated in February 2015, however, apparently because the public no longer supported the idea of sharing senior staff. Archipelago Chief Administrative Officer Stephen Kaegi told a local paper that "[o]ne of the key Carling election issues and the one most talked about was that Carling needed to have their own CAO and their own financial and public works managers" (Phillips 2015). He continued by reiterating what the mayor told council: "his ratepayers told him that Carling should have their own senior staff" (Phillips 2015). Public support is thus a crucial factor in the calculus of cooperation and a reminder that these types of interlocal arrangements not only need administrative support but political support as well.

Conclusion

What does all of this tell us about local government in Canada? Canadian municipalities cooperate and contract with their peers, but certainly not to the extent we see elsewhere in the world. Even so, interlocal contractual and cooperative agreements exist across the country, and from the survey data gathered for this project it is clear local actors have an appetite to continue exploring the potential benefits of these arrangements. These relationships come in a variety of forms and with various states of success. Some have been in place for decades and by all accounts are successful and beneficial. Others were terminated, leaving local relationships in ruins. The quality and availability of important services such as water, waste disposal, and transportation are vital to the health of any community. This book has highlighted the importance of interlocal contracting and service sharing in these and other areas of municipal government. In so doing, it has shone additional light on a servicing practice that is not widely understood. Studying interlocal cooperation provides more clarity about alternatives in service delivery and institutional design. Much of the scholarly attention in Canada has focused on privatization and institutional consolidation. Collaborating with neighbouring governments ought to be included as well. To examine alternatives in service delivery, researchers and practitioners alike need an accurate appraisal of the available options.

The dialogue about servicing efficiency and design is ongoing. This book presents a simple entry point into the field of interlocal cooperation in Canada, but much more work is to be done. The research presented here gives us the impression of municipal administrators and politicians when it comes to their current and potential intergovernmental agreements, but it would be useful to evaluate the effectiveness of these agreements. For instance, the survey data used in this project show that many believe their agreements save money and increase service quality. These claims remain untested in the Canadian context, mostly because information about specific relationships is not readily available. As mentioned in Chapter 2, it took over a year to assemble the data necessary simply to examine agreement components. Convincing municipalities to provide additional data and to examine cost savings and service quality in a longitudinal nature might prove exceedingly difficult, but it is no doubt necessary to enhance the understanding of alternative servicing arrangements. Additionally, definitions of what constitutes service quality are in dispute or could change based upon the community in question. With that said, there remains value in pursuing both ends. Those interviewed for this book indicated they were eager to obtain data related to agreement efficiency and costs. Both the academic and practitioner communities would welcome such a study.

From the standpoint of practitioners, much more needs to be done to increase transparency and accountability in interlocal relationships. Far too little information about interlocal contracting and service sharing is available to the public. While few members of the public are likely clamouring for details about contractual relationships relating to servicing in their communities, some undoubtedly have an interest, and they deserve an opportunity to evaluate these relationships. Provincial governments can help in this task, providing more information about interlocal contracting and service delivery to both the public and municipal administrators.

Far too little attention has been paid to cooperative and service-sharing relationships between Canadian municipalities. We know these relationships exist; we know they involve crucial services for our communities. It is time we devote more attention to their scope and operations.

Appendix

Composition of Census Metropolitan Areas Included in Study

Census Metropolitan Area	Municipalities
Calgary	*Cities*: Airdrie, Calgary *Municipal District*: Rocky Mountain County *Towns*: Chestermere, Cochrane, Crossfield, Irricana *Village*: Beiseker *Hamlet*: Langdon
Edmonton	*Cities*: Edmonton, Fort Saskatchewan, Leduc, St Albert, Spruce Grove *Specialized Municipality*: Strathcona County *Municipal Districts*: Leduc County, Parkland County, Sturgeon County *Towns*: Beaumont, Bon Accord, Bruderheim, Calmar, Devon, Gibbons, Legal, Morinville, Redwater, Stoney Plain *Villages*: Spring Lake, Thorsby, Wabamun, Warburg *Summer Villages*: Betula Beach, Golden Days, Itaska Beach, Kapasiwin, Lakeview, Point Allison, Seba Beach, Sundance Beach
Regina	*City*: Regina *Regional Municipalities*: Edenwold No. 158, Lumsden No. 189, Sherwood No. 159 *Towns*: White City, Pilot Butte, Balgonie, Regina Beach *Villages*: Grand Coulee, Pense, Buena Vista, Pense No. 160, Edenwold, Disley, Belle Plaine *Resort Village*: Lumsden Beach
Saskatoon	*Cities*: Martensville, Saskatoon, Warman *Towns*: Allan, Asquith, Colonsay, Dalmeny, Delisle, Dundurn, Langham, Osler *Villages*: Borden, Bradwell, Clavet, Elstow, Meacham, Vanscoy *Resort Villages*: Shields, Thode *Rural Municipalities*: Blucher No. 343, Colonsay No. 342, Corman Park No. 344, Dundurn No. 313, Vanscoy No. 345.

(*Continued*)

114   Appendix

Composition of Census Metropolitan Areas Included in Study (*continued*)

Census Metropolitan Area	Municipalities
Winnipeg	*City*: Winnipeg *Towns*: Ritchot, Taché, Springfield, East St Paul, West St Paul, Rosser, St François Xavier, Headingley, St Clements
Toronto	*Cities*: Toronto, Mississauga, Brampton, Vaughan *Regional Governments*: Peel Region, Halton Region, York Region, Durham Region *Towns*: Markham, Richmond Hill, Oakville, Ajax, Pickering, Milton, Newmarket, Caledon, Halton Hills, Aurora, Georgina, Whitchurch-Stouffville, New Tecumseth, Bradford West Gwillimbury, Orangeville, East Gwillimbury, Mono *Townships*: Uxbridge, King
Vancouver	*Cities*: Vancouver, Surrey, Burnaby, Richmond, Coquitlam, New Westminster, Port Coquitlam, North Vancouver, Port Moody, Langley, White Rock, Pitt Meadows *District Municipalities*: Langley, Delta, North Vancouver, Maple Ridge, West Vancouver *Villages*: Lions Bay, Belcarra, Anmore
Moncton	*Cities*: Moncton, Dieppe *Town*: Riverview *Parishes*: Moncton, Coverdale, Hillsborough, Elgin, Saint-Paul, Dorchester *Villages*: Memramcook, Salisbury, Hillsborough, Dorchester *Indian Reserve*: Fort Folly 1
Ottawa-Gatineau	*Cities*: Ottawa, Clarence-Rockland *Canton*: Lochaber-Partie-Ouest *Ville*: Gatineau *Municipalités*: Pontiac, Bristol *Towns*: Mississippi Mills, Arnprior *Townships*: North Dundas, Russell, Montague, Beckwith, McNab/Braeside *Municipalities*: The Nation, North Grenville *Village*: Merrickville-Wolford
Saint John	*City*: Saint John *Parishes*: Simonds, Musquash, Westfield, Kingston *Towns*: Grand Bay-Westfield, Rothesay
St John's	*Cities*: St John's, Mount Pearl *Towns*: Conception Bay South, Portugal Cove-St Philip's, Torbay, Logy Bay-Middle Cove-Outer Cove, Paradise, Petty Harbour-Maddox Cove, Bay Bulls *Subdivision of Unorganized*: Division No. 1, Subd. D
Thunder Bay	*City*: Thunder Bay *Municipalities*: Oliver Paipoonge, Neebing *Townships*: Shuniah, Conmee, O'Connor, Gillies *Indian Reserve*: Fort William 52

Notes

1. Introduction

1 The names of these ministers vary, but their purpose is generally consistent across the country.
2 Small sums come from investments and a miscellaneous collection of amusement taxes, licences and permits, and fines and penalties; for more information, see Kitchen (2002).
3 For more information on the Ostromian perspective on polycentricity, see Aligica and Boettke (2009).
4 This survey was distributed by the Laurier Institute for the Study of Public Opinion and Policy at Wilfrid Laurier University. The author would like to thank Jason Roy and Andrea Perella for their help in crafting and distributing the survey. The questionnaire was approved by the Wilfrid Laurier University Research Ethics Board (REB #4501), and distributed using a contact list provided by the Association of Municipal Managers, Clerks, and Treasurers of Ontario. In total, the survey was distributed to 4,068 contacts.
5 Of the 409 municipalities that responded, 378 municipalities (92.4 per cent) indicated that they shared services of some kind. Only 31 municipalities (7.6 per cent) did not cooperate formally with other municipalities. The author would like to thank the ministry for graciously providing access to the survey data.

2. Mapping the Cooperative Landscape

1 While some Indigenous band governments are included in certain CMAs, they are not included in this study. This is not to indicate they are insignificant actors in local governance, but since these governments have a much different structure and many different responsibilities than a

traditional local government, it was decided to exclude them. For more information on interlocal cooperation between municipalities and Indigenous band governments, see Alcantara and Nelles (2014); Nelles and Alcantara (2011).
2 The agreements included in this study were provided directly from municipalities. Best efforts were taken to ensure the accuracy in count and content, but ultimately it was not possible to verify independently the number of agreements from each municipality.
3 Many Canadian provinces have undertaken rounds of policy downloading, transferring certain policy responsibility for certain services to municipalities. For example, in the late 1990s, Ontario downloaded responsibility for the delivery and funding of social services to municipalities and uploaded the costs for education, significantly rebalancing the policy relationship between the two levels of government.
4 These informal agreements also might not be widely known inside the organization, but only to those directly related to the policy area.
5 Only four (or 3 per cent) of the agreements for Toronto predate the city's 1998 amalgamation.
6 The region of Ottawa-Carleton had eleven lower-tier municipalities: the Cities of Ottawa, Nepean, Kanata, Gloucester, Vanier, and Cumberland, the former Townships of West Carleton, Goulbourn, Rideau, and Osgoode, and the former Village of Rockcliffe Park.
7 Most of the categories included in the list are self-explanatory, although some might require elaboration: "Emergency services" encompasses all areas of emergency planning or delivery, such as fire protection, despatch, or reporting; "Transportation" includes road construction, maintenance, snow removal, and the provision of public transportation services; "Waste" includes all landfill services, collection, and maintenance or recycling programming; and, finally, "Administrative" includes all items relating to staffing or other uncategorized maintenance, such as information technology maintenance and sharing.
8 Penetanguishene and Midland have an established history of cooperation and shared a building services department for the better part of a decade prior to the creation of this particular arrangement. Both mayors and chief administrative officers reported a positive working relationship. For more information, see Dunning (2015).
9 Each province has legislation relating to freedom of information requests. The regulations vary, but for the most part, governments are required to grant access to documentation upon request within a prescribed period of time (mostly thirty days). Governments may request additional time if they feel the request is too onerous or the documentation will take additional time to gather. Generally, an initial fee (usually $5.00) applies when

making such requests; a fee is also usually applied to cover the costs of gathering and copying the requested documentation.

10 A number of authors (Kitchen and Slack 2003; O'Brien 1994; Slack 1993, 1997) have also argued that intermunicipal cooperation blurs the lines of local accountability, as those monitoring and executing agreements are often preoccupied with work in their own municipality. Additionally, it is often argued that consumers and taxpayers should know who is accountable for service provision and the taxes or user fees associated with such services.

11 Unlike in other CMAs, in Montreal 138 of the agreements (or roughly 65 per cent) involved the central city. Of course, this figure is likely higher because we were unable to gather agreements from the entire CMA.

12 In certain jurisdictions, such as Ontario, the provincial government mandates municipalities to provide social services. In these cases, these policy areas would be considered necessary.

13 A distinction needs to be made in the "necessary" policy category, as some policy areas are necessary because the province requires them and others because they are necessary for the functioning of the municipality. Within the "necessary" policy area are services, such as planning, that are still delivered with a degree of provincial authority. Here, the provinces mandate that municipalities provide planning services, but do not have strong requirements concerning how the service is to be delivered. This degree of independence differentiates such a policy area from the "mandated" category. On the other hand, roads and transportation are necessary in that sense that the electorate demands them. A municipality cannot function without a network of roads. When it reaches a certain size, it cannot function without a public transportation system.

14 The Ontario Ministry of Municipal Affairs and Housing 2013 survey is evidence that the province's position on interlocal cooperation has changed substantially in the years since *Patterns for the Future* was released.

3. Explaining Cooperation

1 Alcantara and Nelles (2009) do an excellent job elaborating on this conceptualization, discussing both conditions to a larger extent than this book does.

2 When discussing the relationship between shared delivery and efficiency, Holzer and Fry (2011, 81), find that "the literature was disappointingly skimpy on estimating cost savings for different service delivery options."

3 Dijkgraaf and Gradus (2014) find marginal cost savings, but the difference is not statistically significant. Bel and Warner (2015) argue this might be due to the tendency of differences between institutional forms of

delivery to disappear after controlling for the pricing system (in this case, unit-pricing).
4 York Region and Toronto have an agreement for water servicing, overcoming York's distance from Lake Ontario and adequate sources of water.
5 A growing trend in this area is to contract with platform-economy companies, such as Uber. The small but growing town of Innisfil (population 36,000), south of Barrie and about an hour's drive north of Toronto, has recently partnered with Uber to provide subsidized rides to residents instead of starting its own transit system. See Pelley (2017); Spicer (2021).
6 Mandated cooperation can be challenging, and the CMSM case is just one example. For more information on arbitration cases and their outcomes and their long-term impact on affected municipalities, see Spicer (2015a).
7 It should be noted that some of these early public administration theorists did concern themselves with the partitioning of local authority and the subsequent impact on parochialism and associated competitive behaviour. Woodrow Wilson was one such thinker. In one of his earlier works, he argued that "the more power is divided the more irresponsible it becomes" ([1885] 1956, 60). Much of this early conceptualizing regarding fragmented authority informed the works of later consolidationist thinkers.
8 Some recent consolidationist thinking has focused on the amalgamation of local governments as a method of overcoming local urban segregation (see Rusk 1999, 2003).
9 For an interesting case study in local competition regarding image building, see Lehr and Zubrycki's (2012) chapter on Winkler and Morden, Manitoba, in Harvey and Young's *Image Building in Canadian Municipalities* (2012).
10 Some of these efforts might have additional benefits. Richard Florida's work on the "creative class" tells us that there is a correlation between metropolitan growth and success and openness to immigration, artists, members of the LGBT community, and racial integration. In sum, there is a cultural aspect to the growth equation, meaning that the promotion of a more tolerant community might well also have important economic consequences. See Florida (2005).
11 It should be noted that Logan and Molotch (1987, 34–5) see competition as both an internal and an external process. Groups of local boosters often will do what they can to enhance the position of a city to attract scarce mobile capital, but local business owners will still compete with each other within the locality.
12 It should be noted, however, that other factors, such as geography, can both help and hinder this process. For example, a municipality located closer to a lake or river might be more attractive to certain potential residents than one located more inland.

13 The City of London is separated from Middlesex County, meaning that it has no institutional connection to the area around it. For more information on city-county separation, see Spicer (2016a).
14 See the Southern Ontario Marketing Alliance (n.d.) for more information, including operations, membership, and governance.
15 Some of the information in this section comes from an interview conducted with officials from Toronto Water, the City of Toronto department responsible for water and waste-water servicing.
16 The original agreement was signed between York Region and Metropolitan Toronto. The agreement was amended to include the City of Toronto after Metropolitan Toronto underwent a wholesale amalgamation in 1997.
17 This and the following paragraph are based on the author's interview with a City of Toronto official.

4. Agreement Failure and Non-cooperation

1 Due to the research ethics approval for this project, the names of those interviewed cannot be released. However, the individual who participated in the interview from each community is a senior administrative of political official with direct knowledge of the agreement in question.
2 The grant also required that one-third of the funding come from the provincial government and the remaining one-third from the federal government.
3 The Jack Burger Sports Complex was constructed in 1978. It hosts a 1,200-seat area, a 25-metre pool, a therapy pool, and a whirlpool. The facility was renovated in 2015.
4 The agreement is currently being renegotiated and might end up with a new cost-sharing formula.

5. The Role of the Provinces

1 All municipalities have agreed to be part of the regional districts, partly as a result of encouragement by the provincial government. Most, however, have determined that the benefits of membership do outweigh the costs or associated risks. For the most part, municipalities report a positive experience with the regional districts.
2 The City of Abbotsford is a member of only the GVRD parks function. For more information on the membership of the GVRD, see Metro Vancouver (n.d.).
3 Approximately fifty water agreements created with the advent of the Greater Vancouver Water District predate the GVRD and are still in force. Some date back to 1925, and were created with 999-year leases.

4 This interest in shared services is a large reversal of the province's previous position. For example, in a 1987 government report entitled *Patterns for the Future*, the province described the use of interlocal agreements as problematic. Noting that interlocal agreements can be "time-consuming to negotiate, can foster dispute, and can create confusion about accountability," the report argued that they create uncertainty about the lines of policy-making responsibility (Ontario 1987, 62). Interlocal agreements, the report continued, do not necessarily provide for stable administration since their terms and conditions are subject to periodic re-negotiation (65).
5 A number of guides also exist as web resources. See, for instance, the intermunicipal cooperation section on the Alberta Urban Municipalities Association (n.d.) website.
6 See Municipalities Newfoundland and Labrador (2022).
7 Nova Scotia's shared services guide can be viewed at Nova Scotia (2014).

References

Alberta Association of Municipal Districts and Counties. 2005. *Inter-Municipal Agreement Review.* Calgary: G. Pitman Consulting.
Alberta Association of Municipal Districts and Counties. 2008. *Equitable Economics: Inter-Municipal Finance Partnerships.* Calgary: Acton Consulting.
Alberta Urban Municipalities Association. n.d. "Intermunicipal Cooperation." https://auma.ca/advocacy-services/programs-initiatives/intermunicipal-cooperation.
Alcantara, C., and J. Nelles. 2009. "Claiming the City: Co-operation and Making the Deal in Urban Comprehensive Land Claims Negotiations in Canada." *Canadian Journal of Political Science* 43 (3): 705–27. https://doi.org/10.1017/S0008423909990394
Alcantara, C., and J. Nelles. 2014. "Explaining the Emergence of Indigenous-Local Intergovernmental Relations in Settler Societies: A Theoretical Framework." *Urban Affairs Review* 50 (5): 599–622. https://doi.org/10.1177/1078087413501638
Aligica, P.D., and P.J. Boettke. 2009. *Challenging Institutional Analysis and Development: The Bloomington School.* London: Routledge.
Aligica, P.D., and V. Tarko. 2012. "Polycentricity: From Polanyi to Ostrom, and Beyond." *Governance* 25 (2): 237–62. https://doi.org/10.1111/j.1468-0491.2011.01550.x
Anderson, W. 1925. *American City Government.* New York: Henry Hold and Company.
Andrew, S.A. 2008. "Governance by Agreements: Why Do Local Governments Enter into Multilateral Agreements." Working Group on Interlocal Services Cooperation, Paper 37. Detroit: Wayne State University.
Andrew, S.A. 2009. "Recent Developments in the Study of Interjurisdictional Agreements: An Overview and Assessment." *State and Local Government Review* 41 (2): 143–52. https://doi.org/10.1177/0160323X0904100208

Artibise, A.F.J. 1981. *Prairie Urban Development, 1870-1930*. Ottawa: Canadian Historical Association.

Asheim, B.T., and A. Isaksen. 1997. "Location, Agglomeration and Innovation: Towards Regional Innovation Systems in Norway?" *European Planning Studies* 5 (3): 299–330. https://doi.org/10.1080/09654319708720402

Asworth, G.J., and H. Voogd. 1990. *Selling the City: Marketing Approaches in Public Sector Urban Planning*. London: Bellhaven.

Atkins, P., J. Dewitt, and J. Thangavelu. 1999. *The Emerging Regional Governance Network*. Washington, DC: National Association of Regional Councils and National Academy of Public Administration.

Ayres, S., and P. Davis. 2000. "Welcome to the Party? Inclusion, Mutuality and Difference in the West Midlands Regional Development Agency Network in the UK," Paper presented to the Fourth International Research Symposium on Public Management, Erasmus University, April.

Banfield, E. 1957. "The Politics of Metropolitan Area Organization." *Midwest Journal of Political Science* 1 (1): 77–91. https://doi.org/10.2307/2109013

Batrik, T. 1991. *Who Benefits from State and Local Economic Development Policies?* Kalamazoo, MI: Upjohn Institute.

Begg, I. 1999. "Cities and Competitiveness." *Urban Studies* 36 (5–6): 795–809. https://doi.org/10.1080/0042098993222

Begg, I. 2002. *Urban Competitiveness: Policies for Dynamic Cities*. Bristol: Policy Press.

Bel, G., and A. Costas. 2006. "Do Public Sector Reforms Get Rusty? Local Privatization in Spain." *Journal of Policy Reform* 1 (9): 1–24. https://doi.org/10.1080/13841280500513084

Bel, G., and X. Fageda. 2006. "Between Privatization and Intermunicipal Cooperation: Small Municipalities, Scale Economies and Transaction Costs." *Urban Public Economics Review* 6: 13–31

Bel, G., and X. Fegeda. 2011. "Big Guys Eat Big Cakes: Firm Size and Contracting in Urban and Rural Areas." *International Public Management Journal* 14 (1): 4–26. https://doi.org/10.1080/10967494.2011.547746

Bel, G., and M. Mur. 2009. "Inter-Municipal Cooperation, Privatization and Waste Management Costs: Evidence from Rural Municipalities." *Waste Management* 29 (10): 2772–8. https://doi.org/10.1016/j.wasman.2009.06.002

Bel, G., and M. Warner. 2008. "Does Privatization of Solid Waste and Water Services Reduce Cost? A Review of Empirical Studies." *Resources, Conservation and Recycling* 52 (12): 1337–48. https://doi.org/10.1016/j.resconrec.2008.07.014

Bel, G., and M. Warner. 2015. "Intermunicipal Cooperation and Costs: Expectations and Evidence." *Public Administration* 93 (1): 52–67. https://doi.org/10.1111/padm.12104

Benito, B., J. Solana, and M.R. Morena. 2014. "Explaining Efficiency in Municipal Services Providers." *Journal of Productivity Analysis* 42: 225–39. https://doi.org/10.1007/s11123-013-0358-7

Bickers, K.N. 2005. "The Politics of Interlocal Cooperation: A Theory and a Test." Paper Presented at the Creating Collaborative Communities Conference, Wayne State University, Detroit.

Bickers, K.N., and R.M. Stein. 2004. "Interlocal Cooperation and the Distribution of Federal Grant Awards." *Journal of Politics* 66 (3): 800–22. https://doi.org/10.1111/j.1468-2508.2004.00277.x

Binford, H.C. 1985. *The First Suburbs: Residential Communities on the Boston Periphery, 1815–1860.* Chicago: University of Chicago Press.

Bish, R. 1971. *The Public Economy of Metropolitan Areas.* Chicago: Markham.

Bish, R. 1999. "Regional District Review – 1999: Issues and Interjurisdictional Comparisons, Local Government Institute." LGI Report 8. Victoria: University of Victoria and Government of British Columbia, Ministry of Municipal Affairs, September.

Bish, R. 2000. "Evolutionary Alternatives for Metropolitan Areas: The Capital Region of British Columbia." *Canadian Journal of Regional Science* 23 (Spring): 73–87.

Bish, R. 2001. "Local Government Amalgamations: Discredited Nineteenth-Century Ideals Alive in the Twenty-First." Commentary 150. Toronto: C.D. Howe Institute.

Bish, R. 2002. "Accommodating Multiple Boundaries for Local Services: British Columbia's Local Governance System." Paper prepared for a colloquium at the Workshop in Political Theory and Policy Analysis, LGI Working Paper 7, Indiana University, Bloomington, 21 October.

Bish, R., and E. Clemens. 2008. *Local Government in British Columbia.* Victoria: Union of British Columbia Municipalities.

Bish, R., and J. McDavid. 2016. *Governing Greater Victoria: The Role of Elected Officials and Shared Services.* Vancouver: Fraser Institute.

Bish, R., and V. Ostrom. 1973. *Understanding Urban Government: Metropolitan Reform Reconsidered.* Washington, DC: American Enterprise Institute for Public Policy Research.

Boddy, M., and M. Parkinson. 2004. "Competitiveness, Cohesion and Urban Governance." In *City Matters: Competitiveness, Cohesion and Urban Governance,* ed. M. Boddy and M. Parkinson, 407–32. Bristol: Policy Press.

Bollens, J.C. 1973. "Overlapping Governments." In *Governing Urban America in the 1970s,* ed. W.Z. Hirsch and S. Sonenblum. New York: Praeger.

Bolleyer, N. 2006. "Federal Dynamics in Canada, the United States and Switzerland: How Substates' Internal Organization Affects Intergovernmental Relations." *Publius* 36 (4): 471–502. https://doi.org/10.1093/publius/pjl003

Boorstin, D. 1965. *The Americans: The National Experience*. New York: Random House.
Borgatti, S.P., M.G. Everett, and J.C. Johnson. 2013. *Analyzing Social Networks*. Thousand Oaks, CA: SAGE.
Boyne, G.A. 1998. "Bureaucratic Theory Meets Reality: Public Choice and Service Contracting in US Local Government." *Public Administration Review* 58 (6): 474–84. https://doi.org/10.2307/977575
Bozeman, B. 2007. *Public Values and Public Interest: Counterbalancing Economic Individualism*. Washington, DC: Georgetown University Press.
Bramwell, A., J. Nelles, and D.A. Wolfe. 2008. "Knowledge, Innovation and Institutions: Global and Local Dimensions of the ICT Cluster in Waterloo, Canada." *Regional Studies* 42 (1): 101–16. https://doi.org/10.1080/00343400701543231
Brennan, G., and J.M. Buchanan. 1980. *The Power to Tax: Analytical Foundations of a Fiscal Constitution*. New York: Cambridge University Press.
Brown, T.L. 2008. "The Dynamics of Government-to-Government Contracts." *Public Performance Management Review* 31 (3): 364–86. https://doi.org/10.2753/PMR1530-9576310303
Brown, T.L., and M. Potoski. 2006. "Contracting for Management: Assessing Management Capacity under Alternative Service Delivery Arrangements." *Journal of Policy Analysis and Management* 25 (2): 323–46. https://doi.org/10.1002/pam.20175
Buchanan, J.M., and G. Tullock. 1962. *The Calculus of Consent*. Ann Arbor: University of Michigan Press.
Byrnes, J., and B. Dollery. 2002. "Do Economies of Scale Exist in Australian Local Government? A Review of Research Evidence." *Urban Policy and Research* 20 (4): 391–414. https://doi.org/10.1080/0811114022000032618
Cameron, J.M. 1978. "Ideology and Policy Termination: Restructuring California's Mental Healthy System." In *The Policy Cycle*, ed. J.V. May and A.B. Wildavsky, 301–28. Beverly Hills, CA: SAGE.
Cameron, D., and R. Simeon. 2002. "Intergovernmental Relations in Canada: The Emergence of Collaborative Federalism." *Publius* 32 (2): 49–72. https://doi.org/10.1093/oxfordjournals.pubjof.a004947
Capiral, K. 2015. "Saskatchewan Village Cut Fire Services to Reserve Three Weeks Before Fatal Fire." *Globe and Mail*, 18 February.
Carr, J.B., K. LeRoux, and M. Shrestha. 2009. "Institutional Ties, Transaction Costs and External Service Production." *Urban Affairs Review* 44 (3): 403–27. https://doi.org/10.1177/1078087408323939
Cashaback, D. 2001. "Regional District Governance in British Columbia: A Case Study in Aggregation." Ottawa: Institute on Governance.
Chai, H., and D. Treisman. 2004. "State Corroding Federalism." *Journal of Public Economics* 88 (3–4): 819–43. https://doi.org/10.1016/S0047-2727(02)00220-7

City of London and Middlesex Centre. 2000. *Sewage Treatment Amending Agreement*. 21 June.
Coleman, J.S. 1988. "Social Capital in the Creation of Human Capital." *American Journal of Sociology* 94: 95–120. https://doi.org/10.1086/228943
Cook, K.S., R. Hardin, and M. Levi. 2005 *Cooperation Without Trust?* New York: Russell Sage Foundation.
Cooper, P.J. 2003. *Governing by Contract: Challenges and Opportunities for Public Managers*. Washington, DC: CQ Press.
Dachis, B. 2010. "Picking Up Savings: The Benefits of Competition in Municipal Waste Services." Commentary 308. Toronto: C.D. Howe Institute.
Daniels, M.R. 1995. "Organizational Termination and Policy Continuation: Closing the Oklahoma Public Training Schools." *Policy Science* 28: 301–16 https://doi.org/10.1007/BF01000291
Daniels, M.R. 1997. "Symposium: Public Policy and Organizational Termination." *International Journal of Public Administration* 20 (12): 2043–66. https://doi.org/10.1080/01900699708525286
Deas, I., and B. Giordano. 2002. "Locating the Competitive City in England." In *Urban Competitiveness: Policies for Dynamic Cities*, ed. I. Begg, 191–210. Bristol: Policy Press.
DeLeon, P. 1983. "Policy Evaluation and Program Termination." *Review of Policy Research* 2 (4): 631–47. https://doi.org/10.1111/j.1541-1338.1983.tb00793.x
Dijkgraaf, E., and R.H.J.M. Gradus. 2013. "Cost Advantage Cooperations Larger than Private Waste Collectors." *Applied Economics Letters* 20 (7): 702–5. https://doi.org/10.1080/13504851.2012.732682
Dijkgraaf, E., and R.H.J.M. Gradus. 2014. "Waste Management in the Netherlands." In *Handbook on Waste Management*, ed. T. Kinnaman and K. Takeuchi, 287–315. Cheltenham, UK: Edward Elgar.
Dollery, B., B. Grant, and M. Kortt. 2012. *Councils in Cooperation: Shared Services and Australian Local Government*. Sydney: Federated Press.
Dollery, B., and A. Johnston. 2005. "Enhancing Efficiency in Australian Local Government: An Evaluation of Alternative Models of Municipal Governance." *Urban Policy and Research* 23 (13): 73–85. https://doi.org/10.1080/0811114042000335278
Donahue, J.D. 1989. *The Privatization Decision: Public Ends, Private Means*. New York: Basic Books.
Downs, A. 1994. *New Visions for Metropolitan America*. Washington, DC: Brookings Institution Press.
Doz, Y.L. 1996. "The Evolution of Cooperation in Strategic Alliances: Initial Conditions or Learning Processes?" *Strategic Management Journal* 17 (1): 55–83. https://doi.org/10.1002/smj.4250171006
Duffy, H. 1995. *Competitive Cities: Succeeding in the Global Economy*. London: E. & F.N. Spon.

Dunning, J. 2015. "Here's what Midland and Penetanguishene Save by Sharing a Fire Chief." *Simcoe.com*, 21 July.
Eisinger, P. 1989. *The Rise of the Entrepreneurial State: State and Local Economic Development Policy in the United States*. Madison: University of Wisconsin Press.
Federation of Canadian Municipalities. 2011. *First Nations – Municipal Community Infrastructure Partnership Program*. Ottawa: Federation of Canadian Municipalities.
Feiock, R.C. 2002. "A Quasi-Market Framework for Local Economic Development Competition." *Journal of Urban Affairs* 24 (2): 123–42. https://doi.org/10.1111/1467-9906.00118
Feiock, R.C. 2007. "Rational Choice and Regional Governance." *Journal of Urban Affairs* 29 (1): 47–63. https://doi.org/10.1111/j.1467-9906.2007.00322.x
Feiock, R.C. 2013. "The Institutional Collective Action Framework." *Policy Studies Journal* 41 (3): 397–425. https://doi.org/10.1111/psj.12023
Feiock, R.C., A. Steinacker, and H. Park. 2009. "Institutional Collective Action and Economic Development Joint Ventures." *Public Administration Review* 69 (2): 256–70. https://doi.org/10.1111/j.1540-6210.2008.01972.x
Ferris, J. 1986. "The Decision to Contract Out: An Empirical Analysis." *Urban Affairs Quarterly* 22 (2): 289–311. https://doi.org/10.1177/004208168602200206
Fischel, W.A. 2001. *The Homevoter Hypothesis: How Home Values Influence Local Government Taxation, School Finance and Land-Use Policies*. Cambridge, MA: Harvard University Press.
Florida, R. 2005. *Cities and the Creative Class*. New York: Routledge.
Florida, R. 2012. *The Rise of the Creative Class – Revisited and Expanded*. New York: Basic Books.
Fominoff, L. 2018. "City Signs on to 2017 Southern Alberta Emergency Management Resource Sharing Agreement." *Lethbridge News Now*, 21 February.
Foran, M. 2009. *Expansive Discourses: Urban Sprawl in Calgary, 1945-1978*. Edmonton: Athabasca University Press.
Found, A. 2012. *Economies of Scale in Fire and Police Services in Ontario*. IMFG Papers on Municipal Finance and Governance 12. Toronto: University of Toronto, Institute on Municipal Finance and Governance.
Fox, W.F., and T. Gurley. 2006. "Will Consolidation Improve Sub-National Governments?" Policy Research Working Paper 3913. Washington, DC: World Bank, Poverty Reduction and Economic Management, Public Sector Governance Group, May.
Frantz, J.E. 1997. "The High Cost of Policy Termination." *International Journal of Public Administration* 20 (12): 2097–119. https://doi.org/10.1080/01900699708525288
Frederickson, H.G. 1999. "The Repositioning of American Public Administration." *Political Science & Politics* 32 (4): 701–12. https://doi.org/10.2307/420159

Frisken, F. 2001. "The Toronto Story: Sober Reflections on Fifty Years of Experiments with Regional Governance." *Journal of Urban Affairs* 23 (5): 513–41. https://doi.org/10.1111/0735-2166.00104

Frisken, F. 2007. *The Public Metropolis: The Political Dynamics of Urban Expansion in the Toronto Region, 1924–2003*. Toronto: Canadian Scholars' Press.

Fyfe, S. 1975. "Local Government Reform in Ontario." In *Urban Problems Revised*, ed. R.C. Bryfogle and R.R. Krueger. Toronto: Holt, Rinehart and Winston of Canada.

Garcea, J. 2005. "Saskatchewan's Municipal Reform Agenda: Plethora of Processes and Proposals but Paucity of Products." In *Municipal Reform in Canada: Reconfiguration, Re-Empowerment and Rebalancing*, ed. J. Garcea and E. Lesage Jr. Toronto: Oxford University Press.

Garrone, P., L. Grilli, and X. Rousseau. 2013. "Management Discretion and Political Interference in Municipal Enterprises: Evidence from Italian Utilities." *Local Government Studies* 39 (4): 514–40. https://doi.org/10.1080/03003930.2012.726198

Glaab, C.N. 1962. *Kansas City and the Railroads*. Madison: State Historical Society of Wisconsin.

Goetz, E.G., and T. Kayser. 1993. "Competition and Cooperation in Economic Development: A Study of the Twin Cities Metropolitan Area." *Economic Development Quarterly* 7 (1): 63–78. https://doi.org/10.1177/089124249300700106

Goertz, G. 2007. *Social Science Concepts: A User's Guide Exercises*. Princeton, NJ: Princeton University Press.

Gold, J.R., and S.V. Ward. 1994. *Place Promotion: The Use of Publicity and Marketing to Sell Small Towns and Regions*. Chichester, UK: Wiley.

Gordon, R.H. 1983. "An Optimal Taxation Approach to Fiscal Federalism." *Quarterly Journal of Economics* 98 (4): 567–86. https://doi.org/10.2307/1881778

Graddy, E., and B. Chen. 2006. "Influences on the Size and Scope of Networks for Social Service Delivery." *Journal of Public Administration Research and Theory* 16 (4): 533–52. https://doi.org/10.1093/jopart/muj005

Graddy, E., and K. Ye. 2008. "When Do We 'Just Say No'? Policy Termination Decisions in Local Hospital Services." *Policy Studies Journal* 36 (2): 219–42. https://doi.org/10.1111/j.1541-0072.2008.00263.x

Graefe, P., J. Simmons, and L.A. White. 2013. *Overpromising and Underperforming? Understanding and Evaluating New Intergovernmental Accountability Regimes*. Toronto: University of Toronto Press.

Graham, K.A.H., and C. Andrew. 2014. *Canada in Cities: The Politics and Policy of Federal-Local Governance*. Montreal; Kingston, ON: McGill-Queen's University Press.

Graham, K.A.H., and S.D. Phillips. 1998. "'Who Does What' in Ontario: The Process of Provincial-Municipal Disentanglement." *Canadian Public Administration* 41 (2): 175–209. https://doi.org/10.1111/j.1754-7121.1998.tb01536.x

Graham, S. 2002. "Bridging Urban Digital Divides? Urban Polarisation and Information and Communication Technologies (ICTs)." *Urban Studies* 39 (1): 33–56. https://doi.org/10.1080/00420980220099050

Gulati, R., and M. Gargiulo. 1999. "Where Do Interorganizational Networks Come From?" *American Journal of Sociology* 104 (5): 1439–93. https://doi.org/10.1086/210179

Gulati, R., and H. Singh. 1998. "The Architecture of Cooperation: Managing Coordination Costs and Appropriation Concerns in Strategic Alliances." *Administrative Science Quarterly* 43 (4): 781–814. https://doi.org/10.2307/2393616

Gulick, L.H. 1962. *The Metropolitan Problem and American Ideas*. New York: Alfred A. Knopf.

Hanneman, R.A., and M. Riddle. 2005. *Introduction to Social Network Methods*. Riverside: University of California, Riverside.

Harvey, J., and R. Young. 2012. *Image-Building in Canadian Municipalities*. Montreal; Kingston, ON: McGill-Queen's University Press.

Hatley, W.D., R.C. Elling, and J.B. Carr. 2015. "Toward Interlocal Collaboration: Lessons from a Failed Attempt to Create a Fire Authority." In *Municipal Shared Services and Consolidation: A Public Solutions Handbook*, ed. A.C. Henderson. London: Routledge.

Hefetz, A., and M.E. Warner. 2007. "Beyond the Market vs. Planning Dichotomy: Understanding Privatization and its Reverse in US Cities." *Local Government Studies* 33 (4): 555–71. https://doi.org/10.1080/03003930701417585

Hefetz, A., and M.E. Warner. 2012. "Contracting or Public Delivery? The Importance of Service, Market and Management Characteristics." *Journal of Public Administration Research and Theory* 22 (2): 289–317. https://doi.org/10.1093/jopart/mur006

Hefetz, A., M.E. Warner, and E. Vigoda-Gadot. 2014. "Concurrent Sourcing in the Public Sector: A Strategy to Manage Contracting Risk." *International Public Management Journal* 17 (3): 365–86. https://doi.org/10.1080/10967494.2014.935242

Henderson, A.C. 2015. *Municipal Shared Services and Consolidation: A Public Solutions Handbook*. New York: Routledge.

Higgins, D. 1986. "The Process of Reorganizing Local Government in Canada." *Canadian Journal of Political Science* 19 (2): 219–42. https://doi.org/10.1017/S0008423900053993

Hobbs, E.H. 1971. "A Problem: Fragmentation – One Answer: Annexation." *National Civic Review* 60 (8): 427–33. https://doi.org/10.1002/ncr.4100600804

Hodge, G. 2000. *Privatization: An International Review of Performance*. Boulder, CO: Westwood Press.
Hollands, R.G. 2008. "Will the Real Smart City Please Stand Up?" *City* 12 (3): 303–20. https://doi.org/10.1080/13604810802479126
Holzer, M., and J.C. Fry. 2011. *Shared Services and Municipal Consolidation: A Critical Analysis*. Alexandria, VA: Public Technology Institute.
Honadle, B.W. 1984. "Alternative Service Delivery Strategies and Improvement of Local Government Productivity." *Public Productivity Review* 8 (4): 301–13. https://doi.org/10.2307/3379987
Horak, M. 2013. "State Rescaling in Practice: Urban Governance Reform in Toronto." *Urban Research and Practice* 6 (3): 311–28. https://doi.org/10.1080/17535069.2013.846005
Horak, M., and R. Young, eds. 2012. *Sites of Governance: Multilevel Governance and Policy Making in Canada's Big Cities*. Montreal; Kingston, ON: McGill-Queen's University Press.
Hulst, R., and A. van Montfort. 2008. "Intermunicipal Cooperation: A Widespread Phenomenon." In *Intermunicipal Cooperation in Europe*, ed. R. Hulst and A. van Montfort, 1–21. Dordrecht: Springer.
Huxman, C. 1996. *Creating Collaborative Advantage*. London: SAGE.
Isserman, A. 1994. "State Economic Development Policy and Practice in the United States: A Survey Article." *International Regional Science Review* 16 (1–2): 49–100. https://doi.org/10.1177/016001769401600104
Johnson, M., and M. Neiman. 2004. "Courting Business: Competition for Economic Development Among Cities." *Metropolitan Governance: Conflict, Competition and Cooperation*, ed. R.C. Feiock. Washington, DC: Georgetown University Press.
Johnston, J.M., and A.M. Girth. 2012. "Government Contracts and 'Managing the Market': Exploring the Costs of Strategic Management Responses to Weak Vendor Competition." *Administration and Society* 44 (1): 887–900. https://doi.org/10.1177%2F0095399711417396
Jones, V. 1942. *Metropolitan Government*. Chicago: University of Chicago Press.
Kadushin, C. 2012. *Understanding Social Networks: Theories, Concepts and Findings*. New York: Oxford University Press.
Kanareck, A., and M. Baldassare. 1996. "Preferences for State and Regional Planning Efforts among California Mayors and City Planning Directors." *Journal of Planning Education and Research* 16 (2): 93–102. https://doi.org/10.1177/0739456X9601600202
Kaplan, H. 1965. "Politics and Policy-Making in Metropolitan Toronto." *Canadian Journal of Economic and Political Science* 31 (4): 538–51. https://doi.org/10.2307/139829
Keen, M., and M. Marchand. 1997. "Fiscal Competition and the Pattern of Public Spending." *Journal of Public Economics* 66 (1): 333–53. https://doi.org/10.1016/S0047-2727(97)00035-2

Kerr, K. 2018. "Going the Distance: Sudbury East Municipal Association Creates a Model for Sharing Services." *Municipal Monitor*, Fall.

Kiernan, M., and D.C. Walker. 1983. "Winnipeg." In *City Politics in Canada*, ed. W. Magnusson and A. Sancton, 222–54. Toronto: University of Toronto Press.

Kirkpatrick, S.E., J.P. Lester, and M.R. Peterson. 1999. "The Policy Termination Process: A Conceptual Framework and Application to Revenue Sharing." *Policy Studies Review* 16 (1): 209–36. https://doi.org/10.1111/j.1541-1338.1999.tb00847.x

Kitchen, H. 2002. "Canadian Municipalities: Fiscal Trends and Sustainability." *Canadian Tax Journal* 50 (1): 156–80.

Kitchen, H.M., and E. Slack. 2003. "Special Study: New Finance Options for Municipal Governments." *Canadian Tax Journal* 51 (6): 2216–72.

Klijn, E.-H., and G.R. Teisman. 2000. "Governing Public-Private Partnerships: Analysing and Managing the Process and Institutional Characteristics of Public-Private Partnerships." In *Public-Private Partnerships: Theory and Practice in International Perspective*, ed. S.P. Osborne, 84–102. London: Routledge.

Kodrzycki, Y.K. 1998. "Fiscal Pressure and the Privatization of Local Services." *New England Economic Review* (January–February): 39–50.

KPMG. 2013. *Sharing Municipal Services in Ontario: Case Studies and Implications for Ontario Municipalities*. Toronto: KPMG, 3 May.

Kresl, P.K. 1992. *The Urban Economy and Regional Trade Liberalization*. New York: Praeger Press.

Kresl, P.K. 2002. "The Enhancement of Urban Economic Competitiveness." In *Urban Competitiveness: Policies for Dynamic Cities*, ed. I. Begg. Bristol: Policy Press.

Lamonthe, S., and M. Lamonthe. 2016. "Service Shedding in Local Governments: Why Do They Do It?" *Journal of Public Administration Research and Theory* 26 (2): 359–74. https://doi.org/10.1093/jopart/muv012

Leduc County. 2017. *Leduc Regional Fire Services: Conceptual Implementation Plan*. Leduc County, AB: Leduc County.

Lehr, J.C., and K. Zubrycki. 2012. "Image Building in Manitoba." In *Image Building in Canadian Municipalities*, ed. J. Harvey and R. Young, 49–91. Montreal; Kingston, ON: McGill-Queen's University Press.

Leo, C. 2002. "Urban Development: Planning Aspirations and Political Realities." In *Urban Policy Issues*, ed. E.P. Fowler and D. Siegel, 215–36. Toronto: Oxford University Press.

Leo, C., and K. Anderson. 2006. "Being Realistic about Urban Growth." *Journal of Urban Affairs* 28 (2): 169–89. https://doi.org/10.1111/j.0735-2166.2006.00266.x

Leo, C., and W. Brown. 2000. "Slow Growth and Urban Development Policy." *Journal of Urban Affairs* 22 (2): 193–213. https://doi.org/10.1111/0735-2166.00050

LeRoux, K. 2006. *The Role of Structure, Function, and Networks in Explaining Interlocal Service Delivery: A Study of Institutional Cooperation in Michigan*. Detroit: Wayne State University.

LeRoux, K., and J.B. Carr. 2007. "Explaining Local Government Cooperation on Public Works: Evidence from Michigan." *Public Works Management & Policy* 12 (1): 344–58. https://doi.org/10.1177%2F1087724X07302586

LeRoux, K., and S. Pandey. 2011. "City Managers, Career Incentives and Municipal Service Decisions: The Effects of Managerial Ambition on Interlocal Service Delivery." *Public Administration Review* 71 (4): 627–36. https://doi.org/10.1111/j.1540-6210.2011.02394.x

LeSage Jr., E. 2005. "Municipal Reform in Alberta: Breaking Ground at the New Millennium." In *Municipal Reform in Canada: Reconfiguration, Re-Empowerment and Rebalancing*, ed. J. Garcea and E. Lesage Jr., 57–82. Toronto: Oxford University Press.

LeSage Jr., E., M.L. McMillan, and N. Hepburn. 2008. "Municipal Shared Service Collaboration in the Alberta Capital Region: The Case of Recreation." *Canadian Public Administration* 51 (3): 455–73. https://doi.org/10.1111/j.1754-7121.2008.00033.x

Levin, J., and S. Tadelis. 2010. "Contracting for Government Services: Theory and Evidence from US Cities." *Journal of Industrial Economics* 58 (3): 507–41. https://doi.org/10.1111/j.1467-6451.2010.00430.x

Lewis, D.E. 2002. "The Politics of Agency Termination: Confronting the Myth of Agency Immortality." *Journal of Politics* 64 (1): 89–107. https://doi.org/10.1111/1468-2508.00119

Lightbody, J. 1997. "A New Perspective on Clothing the Emperor: Canadian Metropolitan Form, Function and Frontiers," *Canadian Public Administration* 40 (3): 436–56. https://doi.org/10.1111/j.1754-7121.1997.tb01518.x

Logan, J.R., and H.L Molotch. 1987. *Urban Fortunes: The Political Economy of Place*. Berkeley: University of California Press.

Lubell, M., M. Schneider, J.T. Scholz, and M. Mete. 2002. "Watershed Partnerships and the Emergence of Collective Action Institutions." *American Journal of Political Science* 46 (1): 148–63. https://doi.org/10.2307/3088419

Lucy, W.H. 1975. "Metropolitan Dynamics: A Cross-National Framework for Analyzing Public Policy Effects in Metropolitan Areas." *Urban Affairs Quarterly* 11 (2): 155–85. https://doi.org/10.1177/107808747501100201

Lucy, W.H., and D.L. Phillips. 2000. *Confronting Suburban Decline: Strategic Planning for Metropolitan Renewal*. Washington, DC: Island Press.

Lynn, P. 2005. *Mutual Aid: Multijurisdictional Partnerships for Meeting Regional Threats, New Realities: Law Enforcement in the Post-9/11 Era*. Washington, DC: US Department of Justice, Office of Justice Program, Bureau of Justice Assistance.

Magulof, M.B. 1975. "A Modest Proposal for the Governance of America's Metropolitan Areas." *Journal of the American Institute of Planners* 41 (4): 250–7. https://doi.org/10.1080/01944367508977887

Maloney, P. 2011. "City Gives Up $45M to Arva." *London Free Press*, 16 August.

Mankiw, N.G. 2012. "Competition Is Healthy for Governments, Too." *New York Times*, 14 April.

Markusen, A.R. 1984. "Class and Urban Social Expenditure: A Marxist Theory of Metropolitan Government." In *Marxism and the Metropolis*, ed. K.T. Williams and L. Sawers, 82–100. New York: Oxford University Press.

Marvel, M.K., and H.P. Marvel. 2007. "Outsourcing Oversight: A Comparison of Monitoring for In-House and Contracted Services." *Public Administration Review* 67 (3): 521–30. https://doi.org/10.1111/j.1540-6210.2007.00734.x

Marvel, M.K., and H.P. Marvel. 2008. "Government-to-Government Contracting: Stewardship, Agency and Substitution." *International Public Management Journal* 11 (2): 171–92. https://doi.org/10.1080/10967490802095870

Maser, S. 1985. "Demographic Factors affecting Constitutional Decisions: The Case of Municipal Charters." *Public Choice* 47: 122–62. https://doi.org/10.1007/BF00119355

Matkin, D.S., and H.G. Frederickson. 2009. "Metropolitan Governance: Institutional Roles and Interjurisdictional Cooperation." *Journal of Urban Affairs* 31 (1): 45–66. https://doi.org/10.1111/j.1467-9906.2008.00428.x

McDavid, J. 2000. "Alternative Service Delivery in Canadian Local Governments: The Costs of Producing Solid Waste Management Services." *Canadian Journal of Regional Science* 23 (1): 157–74.

McGinnis, M.D. 1999. *Polycentricity and Local Public Economies: Readings from the Workshop in Political Theory and Policy Analysis*. Ann Arbor: University of Michigan Press.

Meder, J., and J.W. Leckrone. 2002. "Hardball: Local Government's Foray into Sports Franchise Ownership." *Journal of Urban Affairs* 24 (3): 353–68. https://doi.org/10.1111/1467-9906.00131

Mendler, A. 2017. "Penetanguishene, Midland Will Continue to Share Fire Chief." *Simcoe.com*, 22 June.

Mertz, E. 2016. "Alberta Introduces Changes to Municipal Government Act." *Global News*, 31 May.

Metro Vancouver. n.d. "Metro Vancouver – Home." http://www.metrovancouver.org/.

MFOA (Municipal Finance Officers Association of Ontario). 2012. *Shared Services in Ontario's Local Public Sector: Localizing Accountability*. Toronto: Municipal Finance Officers Association of Ontario.

Miljan, L., and Z. Spicer. 2015. *Municipal Amalgamation in Ontario*. Vancouver: Fraser Institute.

Mintz, J.M., and T. Roberts. 2006. "Running on Empty: A Proposal to Improve City Finances." Commentary 226. Toronto: C.D. Howe Institute.

Moore, B., and I. Begg. 2004. "Urban Growth and Competitiveness in Britain: A Long-Run Perspective." In *City Matters: Competitiveness, Cohesion and Urban Governance*, ed. M. Boddy and M. Parkinson, 92–109. Bristol: Policy Press.

Morgan, D.R., and M.W. Hirlinger. 1991. "Intergovernmental Service Contracts: A Multivariate Explanation." *Urban Affairs Quarterly* 27 (1): 128–44. https://doi.org/10.1177/004208169102700107

Morin, R., and R. Hanley. 2004. "Community Economic Development in a Context of Globalization and Metropolitization: A Comparison of Four North American Cities." *International Journal of Urban and Regional Research* 28 (2): 369–83. https://doi.org/10.1111/j.0309-1317.2004.00524.x

Municipalities Newfoundland and Labrador. 2022. "COVID-19 Information." http://www.municipalnl.ca/?Content=CCRC/Resources/Case_Studies.

Narula, R. 1999. "Innovating through Strategic Alliances: Moving towards International Partnerships and Contractual Agreements." *Technovation* 19 (5): 283–94. https://doi.org/10.1016/S0166-4972(98)00127-8

Nelles, J. 2009. "Civic Capital and the Dynamics of Intermunicipal Cooperation for Regional Economic Development." PhD thesis, Department of Political Science, University of Toronto.

Nelles, J., and C. Alcantara. 2011. "Strengthening the Ties that Bind? An Analysis of Aboriginal-Municipal Intergovernmental Agreements in Canada." *Canadian Public Administration* 54 (3): 315–34. https://doi.org/10.1111/j.1754-7121.2011.00178.x

Newman, M. 2010. *Networks: An Introduction*. Oxford: Oxford University Press.

Norris, D. 2001. "Prospects for Regional Governance under the New Regionalism: Economic Imperatives versus Political Impediments." *Journal of Urban Affairs* 23 (5): 557–71. https://doi.org/10.1111/0735-2166.00106

Norris, D., D. Phares, and T. Zimmerman. 2009. "Metropolitan Government in the United States? Not Now ... Not Likely." In *Governing Metropolitan Regions in the 21st Century*, ed. D. Phares. London: M.E. Sharpe.

Nova Scotia. 2014. "Regional Service Delivery Cost Sharing Guide." http://novascotia.ca/dma/pdf/mun-RSD-cost-sharing-guide.pdf.

Oakerson, R. 1999. *Governing Local Public Economies: Creating the Civic Metropolis*. Oakland, CA: ICA Press.

Oates, W.E. 1972. *Fiscal Federalism*. New York: Harcourt, Brace and Jovanovich.

Oates, W.E., and R.M. Schwab. 1988. "Economic Competition among Jurisdictions: Efficiency Enhancing or Distortion Inducing?" *Journal of Public Economics* 35 (3): 333–54. https://doi.org/10.1016/0047-2727(88)90036-9

O'Brien, A. 1993. *Municipal Consolidation in Canada and Its Alternatives*. Toronto: Intergovernmental Committee on Urban and Regional Research Press.

Ohemeng, F., and J. Grant. 2008. "When Markets Fail to Deliver: An Examination of Privatization and De-Privatization of Water and Wastewater Services Delivery in Hamilton, Canada." *Canadian Public Administration* 51 (3): 475–99. https://doi.org/10.1111/j.1754-7121.2008.00034.x

Ohlsson, H. 2003. "Ownership and Production Costs: Choosing between Public Production and Contracting Out in the Case of Swedish Refuse Collection." *Fiscal Studies* 24 (4): 451–76. https://doi.org/10.1111/j.1475-5890.2003.tb00091.x

Ontario. 1987. *Patterns for the Future: Report of the Advisory Committee on County Government*. Toronto: Ministry of Municipal Affairs.

Ontario. 1998. *Consolidation of Municipal Services Management: Consolidation Planning Framework: Southern Ontario, January 1998*. Toronto: Government of Ontario.

Osborne, S.P. 2000. *Public-Private Partnerships: Theory and Practice in International Perspective*. London: Routledge.

Ostrom, E. 1972. "Metropolitan Reform: Propositions Derived from Two Traditions." *Social Science Quarterly* 53 (3): 474–93.

Ostrom, E. 1998. "A Behavioral Approach to the Rational Choice Theory of Collective Action: Presidential Address, American Political Science Association, 1997." *American Political Science Review* 92 (1): 1–22. https://doi.org/10.2307/2585925

Ostrom, V., R. Bish, and E. Ostrom. 1988. *Local Government in the United States*. San Francisco: Institute for Contemporary Studies Press.

Ostrom, E., R. Gardiner, and J. Walker. 1994. *Rules, Games and Common-Pool Resources*. Ann Arbor: University of Michigan Press.

Ostrom, E., and J. Walker. 2003. *Trust and Reciprocity: Interdisciplinary Lessons from Experimental Research*. New York: Russell Sage Foundation.

Ostrom, V., and E. Ostrom. 1971. "Public Choice: A Different Approach to the Study of Public Administration." *Public Administration Review* 31 (2): 203–16. https://doi.org/10.2307/974676

Ostrom, V., C. Tiebout, and R. Warren. 1961. "The Organization of Government in Metropolitan Regions: A Theoretical Inquiry." *American Political Science Review* 55 (4): 831–42. https://doi.org/10.2307/1952530

Parkinson, M., and M. Boddy. 2004. "Introduction." In *City Matters: Competitiveness, Cohesion and Urban Governance*, ed. M. Boddy and M. Parkinson, 1–12. Bristol: Policy Press.

Parks, R.B., and R.J. Oakerson. 1989. "Metropolitan Organization and Governance: A Local Public Economy Approach." *Urban Affairs Review* 25 (1): 18–29. https://doi.org/10.1177/004208168902500103

Parsons, D.W. 1995. *Public Policy: An Introduction to the Theory and Practice of Policy Analysis*. Aldershot, UK: Edward Elgar.

Pelley, L. 2017. "Innisfil, Ont., partners with Uber to create substitute for public transit." *CBC News*, 15 May.

Perkmann, M. 2003. "The Rise of the Euroregion: A Bird's Eye Perspective on European Cross-Border Cooperation." Lancaster, UK: Lancaster University, Department of Sociology.

Phares, D. 2009. "Prologue: On Metropolitan Government and Governance." In *Governing Metropolitan Regions in the 21st Century*, ed. D. Phares. London: M.E. Sharpe.

Phillips, P. 2015. "Dissolution of Agreement between Carling and Archipelago." *Parry Sound North Star*, 4 February.

Poitras, J. 2021. "New Brunswick Reforms Merge Dozens of Local Governments and Rural Areas." *CBC News*, 18 November. Online at https://www.cbc.ca/news/canada/new-brunswick/new-brunswick-local-governance-reform-1.6253482.

Post, S. 2002. "Local Government Cooperation: The Relationship between Metropolitan Area Government Geography and Service Provision." Paper presented at the Annual Meeting of the American Political Science Association, Boston, 29 August–1 September.

Post, S. 2004. "Metropolitan Area Governance and Institutional Collective Action." In *Metropolitan Governance: Conflict, Competition and Cooperation*, ed. R.C. Feiock, 67–92. Washington, DC: Georgetown University Press.

Powell, B. 2016. "Canadian Big Cities Need New Revenue Sources: Experts." *Toronto Star*, 27 June.

Qian, Y., and G. Roland. 1998. "Federalism and the Soft Budget Constraint." *American Economic Review* 88 (5): 1143–62. https://www.jstor.org/stable/116864

Reeves, E., and M. Barrow. 2000. "The Impact of Contracting Out on the Costs of Refuse Collection Services: The Case of Ireland." *Economic and Social Review* 31 (2): 129–50

Robbins, M. 2015. *Co-Location and Commercialization: McMaster University's Innovation Park*. Ottawa: Conference Board of Canada.

Robins, G. 2015. *Doing Social Network Research: Network-based Research Design for Social Scientists*. London: SAGE.

Romzek, B.S., and J.M. Johnston. 2002. "Effective Contract Implement and Management: A Preliminary Model." *Journal of Public Administration Research and Theory* 12 (3): 423–53. https://doi.org/10.1093/oxfordjournals.jpart.a003541

Ruggini, J. 2006. "Making Local Government More Workable through Shared Services." *Government Finance Review* 22 (1): 31–5.

Rusk, D. 1999. *Inside Game/Outside Game: Winning Strategies for Saving Urban America*. Washington, DC: Brookings Institution Press.

Rusk, D. 2003. *Cities Without Suburbs*. Washington, DC: Woodrow Wilson Center Press.

Salet, W., A. Thornley, and A. Kreukels. 2003. *Metropolitan Governance and Spatial Planning: Comparative Case Studies of European City Regions*. London: Spon Press.

Sancton, A. 2000. *Merger Mania: The Assault on Local Government*. Montreal; Kingston, ON: McGill-Queen's University Press.

Sancton, A. 2001."Canadian Cities and the New Regionalism." *Journal of Urban Affairs* 23 (5): 543–55. https://doi.org/10.1111/0735-2166.00105

Sancton, A. 2011. *Canadian Local Government: An Urban Perspective*. Don Mills, ON: Oxford University Press.

Sancton, A., R. James, and R. Ramsay. 2000. *Amalgamation vs. Inter-Municipal Cooperation: Financing Local and Infrastructure Services*. Toronto: Intergovernmental Committee on Urban and Regional Research Press.

Saskatchewan Parks and Recreation Association. 2015. *Inter-Municipal Collaboration in Recreation: A Guide for Municipalities in a Growing Province*. Saskatoon: H.J. Linnen Associates.

Savitch, H.V., and R. Vogel. 1996. *Regional Politics: America in a Post-City Age*, Thousand Oaks, CA: SAGE.

Savitch, H.V., and R. Vogel. 2000. "Paths to the New Regionalism." *State & Local Government Review* 32 (3): 158–68. https://doi.org/10.1177/0160323X0003200301

Scheiber, H.N. 1973. "Urban Rivalry and Internal Improvements in the Old Northwest, 1820–1860." In *American Urban History: An Interpretive Reader with Commentaries*, 2nd ed., ed. Alexander Callow Jr. New York: Oxford University Press.

Schneider, M. 1989. *The Competitive City: The Political Economy of Suburbia*. Pittsburgh: University of Pittsburgh Press.

Schnurer, E. 2013. "What Would It Mean for Governments to Compete Like Businesses?" *Atlantic*, 22 May.

Scott, J. 2012. *Social Network Analysis*. New York: SAGE.

Sher, J. 2012. "Cash gauntlet thrown at London: Middlesex County is demanding the city pay $2.37 million more for social housing, which would make a tax freeze even tougher next year." *London Free Press*, 7 May.

Shrestha, M. 2005. "Inter-Local Fiscal Cooperation in the Provision of Local Public Services – The Case of Large US Cities." Presented at the annual meeting of the American Society for Public Administration, Milwaukee, WI, 2–5 April.

Shrestha, M. 2010. "Do Risk Profiles of Services Alter Contractual Patterns? A Comparison Across Multiple Metropolitan Services." In *Self-Organizing*

Federalism: Collaborative Mechanisms to Mitigate Institutional Collective Action, ed. R.C. Feiock and J.T. Scholz, 114–41. Cambridge: Cambridge University Press.

Shrestha, M., and R. Feiock. 2007. "Interlocal Cooperation in the Supply of Local Public Goods: A Transaction Cost and Social Exchange Explanations." Working Group on Interlocal Services Cooperation, Paper 29. Detroit: Wayne State University.

Shrestha, M., and R. Feiock. 2009. "Governing U.S. Metropolitan Areas: Self-Organizing and Multiplex Service Networks." *American Politics Research* 37 (4): 801–23. https://doi.org/10.1177/1532673X09337466

Siegel, D. 2005. "Municipal Reform in Ontario." In *Municipal Reform in Canada: Reconfiguration, Re-Empowerment and Rebalancing,* ed. J. Garcea and E.C. Lesage Jr., 20–69. Toronto: Oxford University Press.

Siekierska, A. 2018. "Innisfil, Ontario sticks with its Uber-as-public-transit plan, extending its pilot project." *Financial Post,* 15 March.

Simões, P., N. Cruz, and R.C. Marques. 2012. "The Performance of Private Partners in the Waste Sector." *Journal of Cleaner Production* 29–30 (July): 214–21. https://doi.org/10.1016/j.jclepro.2012.01.027

Slack, E. 1993. "Comments on Efficiency of Delivering Local Government Services under Alternative Organizational Modes." In *Competitiveness and Delivery of Public Services,* ed. R. Crowley. Kingston: Queen's University, School of Policy Studies, Government and Competitiveness Project.

Slack, E. 1997. *Inter-Municipal Cooperation: Sharing of Expenditures and Revenues.* Toronto: Intergovernmental Committee on Urban and Regional Research Press.

Slack, E., and R. Bird. 2013. *Merging Municipalities: Is Bigger Better?* IMFG Paper 14. Toronto: University of Toronto, Institute on Municipal Finance and Governance.

Smyth, H. 1994. *Marketing the City: Flagship Developments in Urban Regeneration.* London: Spon.

Sorensen, R.J. 2007. "Does Dispersed Public Ownership Impair Efficiency? The Case of Refuse Collection in Norway." *Public Administration* 85 (4): 1045–58. https://doi.org/10.1111/j.1467-9299.2007.00681.x

Southern Ontario Marketing Alliance. n.d. "About SOMA." https://canadasindustrialheartland.com/regional-profile/about-soma.

Spicer, Z. 2014. "Linking Regions, Linking Functions. Inter-Municipal Agreements in Canada." IMFG Perspectives 10. Toronto: University of Toronto, Institute on Municipal Finance and Governance.

Spicer, Z. 2015a. "Adapting (Municipal) Form to (Provincial) Function: City-County Separation and the Introduction of the Consolidated Municipal Service Manager System in Ontario." *American Review of Canadian Studies* 45 (3): 346–64. https://doi.org/10.1080/02722011.2015.1086396

Spicer, Z. 2015b. "Cooperation, Coordination and Competition: Why Do Municipalities Participate in Economic Development Alliances?" *Canadian Public Administration* 58 (4): 549–73. https://doi.org/10.1111/capa.12133

Spicer, Z. 2015c. "Regionalism, Municipal Organization and Inter-Local Cooperation in Canada." *Canadian Public Policy* 41 (2): 137–50. https://doi.org/10.3138/cpp.2014-078

Spicer, Z. 2016a. *The Boundary Bargain: Growth, Development and the Future of City-County Separation*. Montreal; Kingston, ON: McGill-Queen's University Press.

Spicer, Z. 2016b. "Governance by Handshake? Assessing Informal Municipal Service Sharing Relationships." *Canadian Public Policy* 42 (4): 505–13. https://doi.org/10.3138/cpp.2015-079

Spicer, Z. 2017. "Bridging the Accountability and Transparency Gap in Inter-Local Collaboration." *Local Government Studies*. 43 (3): 388–407. https://doi.org/10.1080/03003930.2017.1288617

Spicer, Z. 2021. "A New Public-Private Partnership for the Platform Age? Uber as Public Transit." In *The Platform Economy and the Smart City: Technology and the Transformation of Urban Policy*, ed. A. Zwick and Z. Spicer. Montreal; Kingston, ON: McGill-Queen's University Press.

Spicer, Z., and A. Found. 2016. "Thinking Regionally: How to Improve Service Delivery in Canada's Cities." Commentary 458. Toronto: C.D. Howe Institute

Sproule-Jones, M. 1974. "Citizen Participation in a Canadian Municipality." *Public Choice* 17 (Spring): 73–83. https://www.jstor.org/stable/30023154

Sproule-Jones, M., and K.D. Hart. 1973. "A Public Choice Model of Political Participation." *Canadian Journal of Political Science* 6 (2): 175–94. https://doi.org/10.1017/S0008423900039639

Stein, R. 1990. *Urban Alternatives: Public and Private Markets in the Provision of Local Services*. Pittsburgh: University of Pittsburgh Press.

Steinacker, A. 2004. "Metropolitan Area Governance and Institutional Collective Action." In *Metropolitan Governance: Conflict, Competition and Cooperation*, ed. R. Feiock. Washington, DC: Georgetown University Press.

Stevens, B.J. 1978. "Scale, Market Structure and the Cost of Refuse Collection." *Review of Economics and Statistics* 60 (3): 438–48. https://doi.org/10.2307/1924169

Stolte, E. 2016. "Alberta Forces Cities and Counties to Share Costs for Major Roads and Services." *Edmonton Journal*, 31 May.

Strebel, M.A., and D. Kubler. 2021. "Citizens' Attitudes towards Local Autonomy and Inter-Local Cooperation: Evidence from Western Europe." *Comparative European Politics* 19: 188–207. https://doi.org/10.1057/s41295-020-00232-3

Studenski, P. 1930. *The Government of Metropolitan Areas in the United States*. New York: National Municipal League.

Sullivan, H., and C. Skelcher. 2002. *Working across Boundaries: Collaboration in Public Services*. London: Palgrave Macmillan.
Teles, F. 2016. *Local Governance and Inter-Municipal Cooperation*. London: Palgrave.
Thompson, P., J. Frances, R. Levacic, and J. Mitchell. 1991. *Markets, Hierarchies and Networks: The Co-Ordination of Social Life*. London: SAGE.
Thurmaier, K. 2005. "Elements of Successful Interlocal Agreements: An Iowa Case Study." Working Group on Interlocal Services Cooperation, Paper 2. Detroit: Wayne State University.
Thurmaier, K., and C.H. Wood. 2002. "Interlocal Agreements as Overlapping School Networks: Picket-Fence Regionalism in Metropolitan Kansas City." *Public Administration Review* 62 (5): 585–98. https://doi.org/10.1111/1540-6210.00239
Tiebout, C.M. 1956. "A Pure Theory of Local Expenditures." *Journal of Political Economy* 64 (5): 416–24. https://doi.org/10.1086/257839
Tullock, G. 1965. *The Politics of Bureaucracy*. Washington, DC: Public Affairs Press.
Turok, I. 2005. "Cities, Competition and Competitiveness: Identifying New Connections." In *Changing Cities: Rethinking Urban Competitiveness, Cohesion and Governance*, ed. N. Buck, I. Gordon, A. Harding, and I. Turok. London: Palgrave Macmillan.
Ugboro, I.O., K. Obeng, and W.K. Talley. 2001. "Motivations and Impediments to Service Contracting, Consolidations, and Strategic Alliance in Public Transit Organizations." *Administration & Society* 33 (1): 79–103. https://doi.org/10.1177/00953990122019695
Van Brenk, D. 2011. "Growing Friction Looms on London's Outskirts." *London Free Press*, 7 November.
Vander Ploeg, C.G. 2002. *Big City Revenue Sources: A Canada-US Comparison of Municipal Tax Tools and Revenue Levers*. Calgary: Canada West Foundation.
van Slyke, D. 2003. "The Mythology of Privatization in Contracting for Social Services." *Public Administration Review* 63 (3): 298–315 https://doi.org/10.1111/1540-6210.00291
van Slyke, D., and C.A. Hammonds. 2003. "The Privatization Decision: Do Public Managers Make a Difference?" *American Review of Public Administration* 33 (2): 146–63. https://doi.org/10.1177/0275074003251374
Varady, D.P., and J. Raffel. 1995. *Selling Cities: Attracting Homebuyers through Schools and Housing Programs*. Albany: State University of New York Press.
Visser, J. 2004. "Townships and Nested Governance: Spoilers or Collaborators in Metropolitan Services Delivery." *Public Performance and Management Review* 27 (3): 80–101. https://www.jstor.org/stable/3381147
Vogel, R., and J. Harrington. 2003. *Political Change in the Metropolis*. New York: Longman.

Vojnovic, I. 1998. "Municipal Consolidation in the 1990s: An Analysis of British Columbia, New Brunswick and Nova Scotia." *Canadian Public Administration* 41 (2): 239–83. https://doi.org/10.1111/j.1754-7121.1998.tb01538.x

Wade, R. 1959. *The Urban Frontier: The Rise of Western Cities, 1700–1830.* Cambridge, MA: Harvard University Press.

Walisser, B., G. Paget, and M. Dann. 2013. "New Pathways to Effective Regional Governance: Canadian Reflections." In *New Century Local Government: Commonwealth Perspectives*, ed. G. Samson and P. McKinley, 145–68. London: Commonwealth Secretariat.

Warner, M.E. 2006. "Inter-Municipal Cooperation in the U.S.: A Regional Governance Solution?" *Urban Public Economics Review* 6: 221–39.

Warner, M.E. 2012. "Privatization and Urban Governance: The Continuing Challenges of Efficiency, Voice and Integration." *Cities* 29 (S2): S38–S43. https://doi.org/10.1016/j.cities.2012.06.007

Warner, M.E. 2015. "Municipal Size, Resources and Efficiency: Theoretical Bases for Shared Services and Consolidation." In *Municipal Shared Services and Consolidation: A Public Solutions Handbook*, ed. A. Henderson, 1–14. New York: Routledge.

Warner, M.E., and A. Hefetz. 2002. "Applying Market Solutions to Public Services: An Assessment of Efficiency, Equity and Voice." *Urban Affairs Review* 38 (1): 70–89. https://doi.org/10.1177%2F107808702401097808

Warren, R. 1966. *Government in Metropolitan Regions: A Reappraisal of Fractionated Political Organization.* Davis: University of California, Institute of Governmental Affairs.

Wassenaar, M.C., E. Dijkgraaf, and R.H.J.M. Gradus. 2010. "Contracting Out: Dutch Municipalities Reject the Solution for the VAT Distortion." *Local Government Studies* 36 (5): 617–36. https://doi.org/10.1080/03003930.2010.506976

Wasserman, S., and K. Faust. 1994. *Social Network Analysis: Methods and Applications.* Cambridge: Cambridge University Press.

Williams, O. 1967. "Life-Style Values and Political Decentralization in Metropolitan Areas." *Southwestern Social Science Quarterly* 48 (December): 299–310.

Wilson, W. [1885] 1956. *Congressional Government.* New York: Meridian Books.

Wise, C.R. 1997. "The Future of Public Law: Beyond Administrative Law and National Borders." In *Handbook of Public Law and Administration*, ed. P.J. Cooper and C.A. Newland, 569–87. San Francisco: Jossey-Bass.

Wolfe, A.D., and A. Bramwell. 2008. "Innovation, Creativity and Governance: Social Dynamics of Economic Performance in City-Regions." *Innovation: Management, Policy and Practice* 10 (2–3): 170–82. https://doi.org/10.5172/impp.453.10.2-3.170

Wolfson, J., and F. Frisken. 2000. "Local Response to the Global Challenge: Comparing Local Economic Development Policies in a Regional Context."

Journal of Urban Affairs 22 (4): 361–84. https://doi.org/10.1111/0735-2166.00062

Wolman, H. 2016. "Learning from Abroad: Multi-Purpose Special Districts in British Columbia as a Possible Model for Governance Innovation for Local Governments in the United States." *Local Government Research Collaborative.* Phoenix: Arizona State University.

Wood, C.H. 2005. "The Nature of Metropolitan Governance in Urban America: A Study of Cooperation, Conflict, and Avoidance in the Kansas City Region." Working Group on Interlocal Services Cooperation, Paper 9. Detroit: Wayne State University.

Xuereb, M. 2014. "Municipalities Need Access to More Revenue Sources." *Waterloo Region Record*, 21 October.

Yang, K., J.Y. Hsieh, and T.S. Li. 2009. "Contracting Capacity and Perceived Contracting Performance: Nonlinear Effects and the Role of Time." *Public Administration Review* 69 (4): 681–96. https://doi.org/10.1111/j.1540-6210.2009.02017.x

Young, R. 2012. "Conclusion." In *Image-Building in Canadian Municipalities*, ed. J. Harvey and R. Young, 167–96. Montreal; Kingston, ON: McGill-Queen's University Press.

Zafra-Gómez, J.L., D. Prior, A.M. Plata-Díaz, and A.M. López-Hernández. 2013. "Reducing Costs in Times of Crisis: Delivery Forms in Small and Medium Sized Local Governments' Waste Management Services." *Public Administration* 91 (1): 51–68. https://doi.org/10.1111/j.1467-9299.2011.02012.x

Zeemering, E.S. 2015. "Managing Interlocal Contracts and Shared Service Relationships." In *Municipal Shared Services and Consolidation: A Public Solutions Handbook*, ed. A.C. Henderson. New York: Routledge

Zimmerman, J.F. 1970. "Metropolitan Reform in the U.S.: An Overview." *Public Administration Review* 30 (5): 531–43. https://doi.org/10.2307/974421

Index

The letter *f* following a page number denotes a figure; the letter *t* a table.

access to information requests, 39–40
administration: of contracts, 91–2; of informal agreements, 39; in relationship management, 79; staffing changes, 87–8
administrative services agreements, 32–3, 35, 72–3, 88
agency costs, 16, 77, 109
agreement intensity, 41–4, 45*f*, 103
agreements: adaptive vs. restrictive, 35–8; challenges to forming, 59–60, 106; maintenance of, 91, 92; motivations for, 103–4; provinces' attitudes on, 46; public access to, 38–41, 109, 111; types, 16–20, 102–3. *See also* Census Metropolitan Area (CMA) agreements survey; contracts; failed agreements; interlocal cooperation; *specific places*
Alberta: consolidations, 9, cooperation mandates, 98
Alberta Association of Municipal Districts and Counties, 99
Alcantara, Christopher, 41–2
altruism, 33–4
amalgamations: instances in Canada, 4, 9, 27, 29, 83, 94; and interlocal cooperation, 95, 100, 107; in provincial strategy, 46, 64. *See also* consolidations
Andrew, Simon, 35, 45
Archipelago, The, Ontario, 72–3, 109–10
Arva, Ontario, 71
assessment bases, 67, 68, 71
assumption making: *a priori* and *a posteriori*, 49–50; on cost savings, 51, 54, 103–4
Aurora, Ontario, 4
autonomy: in interlocal agreements, 13, 19; of political leaders, 15

Ben, Richard, 34
binding agreement measurement, 41–2, 43
Bish, Robert, 97
Blucher, Saskatchewan, 73
boosterism, 13, 66
borders and boundaries: as cooperation factor, 56–7, 93, 105; protectiveness over, 69–70
Bowman, Quebec, 30
British Columbia regional districts, 96–8, 100, 107

British North America Act (1867), 8, 93
business activity, 67
buyer and seller model (Schneider), 65–6

Calgary, Alberta, 9, 46, 98
capacity: for cooperative process, 49, 50*t*, 58, 87, 108–9; for service delivery, 52, 72–4
Carling, Ontario, 72–3, 109–10
Carr, Jered B., 45, 80
Census Metropolitan Area (CMA) agreements survey: agreement intensity scores, 43–5; components, 36–7; data collection, 25–8; methodological challenges, 38–41; policy areas, 30–5, 68–70; scope and structure, 46–7; types and volumes, 28–30, 31*f*, 37–8, 102. *See also specific places and policy areas*
Charlton and Dack, Ontario, 85
citizens: in public choice theory, 9–10, 63–4. *See also* public; residents
clauses and components, 36–7, 89, 92
CMA survey. *See* Census Metropolitan Area (CMA) agreements survey
co-managed services, 61
collaboration: in agreement intensity measure, 43; defined, 6; provincial government influences on, 95, 98–100. *See also* interlocal cooperation
commercial activity, 67, 71
commitments: in partner relationships, 59, 78, 90; and termination clauses, 37. *See also* cooperative intensity
common needs, 56, 104–5
communications, 59–60, 79, 108

competition: Canadian vs. US experience, 64–5; expectations and incentives, 62–6, 79; goods categories, 66–8; and policy areas, 68–70, 88, 105, 109; private sector dynamics, 60–1; in selected municipalities, 70–3, 74–5; strategic, 73–4, 105–6; and transaction costs, 51
components and clauses, 36–7, 89, 92
Consolidated Municipal Service Manager (CMSM) program, 52–3, 98
consolidationism, 8–9, 10, 11, 13, 62–3, 64
consolidations, 46, 93. *See also* amalgamations
contracts: characteristics, 18, 35; for emergency services, 32–5; informal vs. formal, 17–18; management, 91–2; structure, 92. *See also* agreements
Cooper, Phillip, 91, 92
cooperation. *See* interlocal cooperation
cooperative intensity measurement, 41, 43–4
coordination costs, 16
costs and cost savings: assumptions about, 51, 54, 103–4; commitments, 59; and economies of scale, 12, 50, 60–1; in fiscal intensity formula, 42; of termination, 90, 107. *See also* transaction costs
council membership: as shared resource, 26*f*; shifts in support, 37, 49, 57*f*, 58, 80

Dann, Michelle, 97
Deep River, Ontario, 86, 87–8
Denholm, Quebec, 30

direct production, 60
dispute resolution mechanisms, 36

economic activity, 67
economic development, 69, 72, 86–7
Edmonton, Alberta, 9, 28, 46, 94, 98
efficiencies: in contract management, 58, 105; in government service delivery, 11, 13, 54, 55, 104; in private sector, 60
Elling, R.C., 80
emergency services, 24–5, 30, 31–5, 41, 70, 73
enforcement costs, 16
Englehart, Ontario, 85
Essa, Ontario, 86
evaluation periods, 92
exchange measurement, 42
expiry clauses, 36, 89
externalities: management of, 12, 52; from shared borders, 57

failed agreements: 2012 survey methodology, 81–2; in administrative issues, 87–8; in capacity issues, 87; in change in legislation, 88; factors, 77–81, 83f, 106; in increase in resources needed, 84–5; in partner disagreements, 82–4; by policy area, 88, 89f; in poor results, 85–7
federal government, 8, 67–8
Federation of Canadian Municipalities, 99
Feiock, R.C., 15
financial disagreements, 59
fire services, 34–5, 73, 81
fiscal health, 58, 78–9, 105, 109
fiscal incentives, 50–1
fiscal intensity, 42
Fischel, William, 64
French River, Ontario, 3–4

Gananoque, Ontario, 87
geographic density, 15
Governing by Contract (Cooper), 91
governments: density of local, 15; distribution of powers, 8; interrelationship studies, 20–3; mandates on cooperation, 52–3, 98–9, 100. *See also* federal government; provincial governments; regional districts
Grandmaître, Bernard, 95
Greater Vancouver Regional District (GVRD), 96–8
group composition, 14–15
growth: competition for, 13, 57, 66, 68, 70–2; control mechanisms, 74–5
growth management boards, 98
guides, 99–100

Halifax, Nova Scotia, 9, 27, 94
Hamilton Township, Ontario, 82–4
Hamilton-Wentworth Region, Ontario, 94
handshake agreements. *See* informal contracts
Hatley, W.D., 80
Head, Clara and Maria, Ontario, 86
home rule, 94, 100
Homevoter Hypothesis, The (Fischel), 64

ideological leanings, 80
industrial activity, 67
informal agreements, 17–18, 28, 39
information sharing, 102
infrastructure, competition for, 67–8
institutional design models, 8–11
institutional integration measurement, 41, 42, 43
intergovernmental relationship studies, 20–3
interlocal cooperation: benefits, 11–13; competitive advantages, 68;

interlocal cooperation (*cont.*)
conditions, 49, 50*t*; in cooperation intensity measurement, 43–4; defined, 6–7; incentives, 50–2; influences on, 13–16, 46; mandatory, 52–3, 98–9, 100, 103; research in Canada, 7, 20–3, 110; risks, 5, 48–9; strategic, 72, 75–6, 105–6. *See also* agreements
intermunicipal collaboration frameworks (ICFs), 98
investments, competition for, 13

James, Rebecca, 39
Johnston, Jocelyn M., 91

Kaegi, Stephen, 110
Killarney, Ontario, 3–4
KPMG service-sharing study, 4

Lamonth, Meeyoung, 78
Lamonth, Scott, 78
land, as competitive advantage, 69–70
Laurentian Hills, Ontario, 86, 87–8
Leduc, Alberta, 33
Leeds and Grenville, Ontario, 87
legislation: British North America Act (1867), 8; and interlocal agreements, 30, 35, 37, 73, 88; Local Service Realignment Act (Ontario 1998), 52; Municipal Government Act (Alberta), 98
LeRoux, Kelly, 45
Lethbridge, Alberta, 33–4
letters of agreement, 35
Local Governance and Inter-Municipal Cooperation (Teles), 49
Local Service Realignment Act (Ontario 1998), 52, 98
Logan, John R., 66
London, Ontario, 70–2
Loon Lake, Saskatchewan, 34–5
Lucy, William H., 65, 73

Makwa Sahgaiehcan First Nation reserve, Saskatchewan, 34–5
mandatory cooperation agreements, 52–3, 98–9, 100, 103
marketing alliances, 72
Markham, Ontario, 4
Markstay-Warren, Ontario, 3–4
Mauro, Joe, 33
McDavid, James, 97
McKellar, Ontario, 85–6
memoranda of understanding, 35
Middlesex County, Ontario, 70–2
Midland, Ontario, 32–3
Millet, Alberta, 5
Molotch, Harvey L., 66
monitoring mechanisms, 36, 74–5, 92
monopolies, 9, 10, 69
Montreal, Quebec, 40–1, 94
Municipal Finance Officers Association of Ontario, 99
Municipal Government Act (Alberta), 98
municipal governments: powers in Canada, 7–8; theories of governance, 8–11. *See also* partnerships; *specific places*
mutual aid agreements, 25, 31, 35, 36, 37

natural resources, 52
negotiation and division costs, 16
Nelles, Jen, 41–2
networks, 11, 19–20, 108
New Brunswick, 9
new regionalism, 11–12
Newfoundland and Labrador, 99
Newmarket, Ontario, 4
Nova Scotia: consolidations, 9; shared services guides, 99–100, 107

Obeng, Kofi, 15
Ontario: attitudes to agreements, 46, 74, 107; consolidations, 9, 93;

cooperation mandates, 52–3, 98;
  Patterns for the Future (report), 46,
  95
Ontario Municipal Affairs and
  Housing survey (2012): data
  collected, 22–3, 24–5, 26f, 102–3;
  follow-up interviews, 81–2, 83f
Ontario municipal officials survey
  (2015): agreement challenges,
  59–60; agreement types, 58–9;
  desired qualities in agreements,
  55–8; reasons to cooperate, 54–5;
  scope, 22, 53–4
oral agreements. *See* informal
  agreements
Ostrom, Elinor, 10
Ottawa-Carleton Region, Ontario,
  29, 94
Ottawa, Ontario, 28–9

Paget, Gary, 97
Parry Sound District, Ontario, 85
partnerships: characteristics,
  19; commitment levels,
  59, 78; in cooperative
  intensity measurement,
  41–4; disagreements, 82–4; per
  agreement, 30; and relationship
  management, 79; selection factors,
  55–8, 104–5
Patterns for the Future (Ontario), 46,
  95
pay-for-service agreements, 34–5, 73
Penetanguishene, Ontario, 32–3
performance issues, 85–8
personnel issues, 80, 87–8
Phillips, David L., 65, 73
Pickering, Ontario, 4
place entrepreneurs, 66
planning services, 70–1, 97
policing, 70
policy areas: competitiveness in,
  68–70; in failed agreements,
88, 89f, in Greater Vancouver
  Regional District, 96–8; in
  intensity measurement, 42, 43; in
  surveyed agreements, 24–5, 30,
  32f, 102–3, 105–6. *See also specific
  policy areas*
political leadership: and ideologies,
  80; and interlocal agreements,
  15, 49, 106; and relationship
  management, 79
political will, 87
polycentrism, 10
populations: in Census Metropolitan
  Areas, 28t, growth, 64–5, 66–7, 68;
  homogeneity, 14–15
Port Hope, Ontario, 82–4, 90
Post, Stephanie, 14
powers: distribution in government,
  8; dynamics between partners, 15
private sector contracts, 18, 60–2
privatization, 18, 51
profit motivation, 33–4, 61
property taxes, 68
provincial governments:
  consolidation activity, 46, 62, 64,
  93–4; decision-making powers, 8,
  10, 93; and interlocal cooperation,
  94–5, 98–100, 107–8, 111; as
  market influencers, 67–8. *See also*
  legislation; *specific provinces*
public: input, 92; support, 81,
  109–10
public choice theory, 9–10, 62–4
public transit, 35, 68

Quebec: consolidations, 9; interlocal
  agreements, 29–30; shared services
  guide, 99

Ramsay, Rick, 39
Regina, Saskatchewan, 9
regional districts, 93–4, 95, 96–9
regionalism, 12–13

relationships: and contract administration, 91, 92; social, 79
reputation, 90, 108
residential developments, 71
residents, 54–5, 63–4, 81. *See also* public
resource sharing agreements, 25, 26*f*, 52
resources: changes to requirements, 84–5; competition for, 67–8. *See also* natural resources
revenues, 8
Richmond Hill, Ontario, 4
risk: in fiscal intensity measurement, 42; in interlocal agreements, 36, 37, 48–9, 103, 106
road maintenance, 24, 30, 36, 54–5, 69
Romzek, Barbara S., 91
rural vs. urban services, 98–9

Sancton, Andrew, 39
Saskatchewan Parks and Recreation Association, 99
Saskatoon, Saskatchewan, 9, 73
Schneider, Mark, 65–6, 69
service sharing agreements, 3–4, 32, 48–9
service shedding, 78
services: in competitive advantages, 69, 70; delivery options, 3, 6; in interlocal agreements, 4, 12, 37, 52–3, 78, 81, 103; provincial authority over, 93; public vs. private delivery, 18, 60–2; rural vs. urban, 98–9. *See also specific policy areas*
Sewell, John, 74
sewer system access agreement, 71
Shrestha, Manoj, 45
Simcoe County, Ontario, 86
Skelcher, Chris, 19
social capital, 14, 90

social services, 70
Southern Alberta Emergency Management Resource Sharing Agreement, 33–4
Southern Ontario Marketing Alliance (SOMA), 72
spatial monopolists, 69
St.-Charles, Ontario, 3–4
staff changes, 59
Sudbury, Ontario, 94
Sullivan, Helen, 19
surveys. *See* Census Metropolitan Area (CMA) survey; Ontario Municipal Affairs and Housing (2012) survey; Ontario municipal officials survey (2015)

Talley, Wayne K., 15
Teles, Filipe, 13, 21, 49
terminations: clauses, 36–7; decision-making, 90–1, 107; process, 89–90
Terry, Dana, 33–4
Teslin, Yukon, 5
Thurmaier, Kurt, 45
Tiebout, Charles M., 9, 64
timing in agreements, 41, 43
Toronto, Ontario: amalgamations, 46; interlocal agreements, 28, 40; as regional district, 93–4; and York Region, 5, 74–5
tourism office agreement, 85–6
transaction costs: influences on, 18, 30, 50–1, 104; types, 15–16, 77–8
transparency, 38–41, 109, 111
transportation, 68–9
trust: as cooperation factor, 26, 46, 108; impact of terminations on, 90; interorganizational, 14, 80, 91; and partner selection, 20, 57, 58, 62, 105
Turcot, Dennis, 4

Ugboro, Isaiah O., 15
United States: interlocal agreements, 45–6; municipalities, 100
Urban Fortunes (Logan and Molotch), 68
urban vs. rural services, 98–9

Vancouver, British Columbia. *See* Greater Vancouver Regional District (GVRD)
Vaughan, Ontario, 4

Walisser, Brian, 97
water services, 52, 74–5
Waterloo Region, Ontario, 67
Wetaskiwin, Alberta, 5
willingness to cooperate, 49, 50*t*
Winnipeg, Manitoba, 9, 46, 94
Wise, Charles, 91
Wood, Curtis H., 45

York Region, Ontario, 5, 74–5

Lightning Source UK Ltd.
Milton Keynes UK
UKHW011314291122
413059UK00019B/185/J